the rain parade

A Photographic Journey Across Ghana

Words & Images by Julia Blaukopf

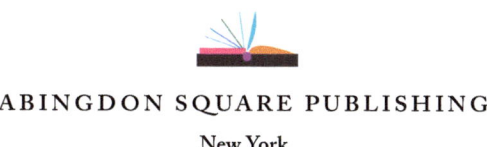

ABINGDON SQUARE PUBLISHING

New York

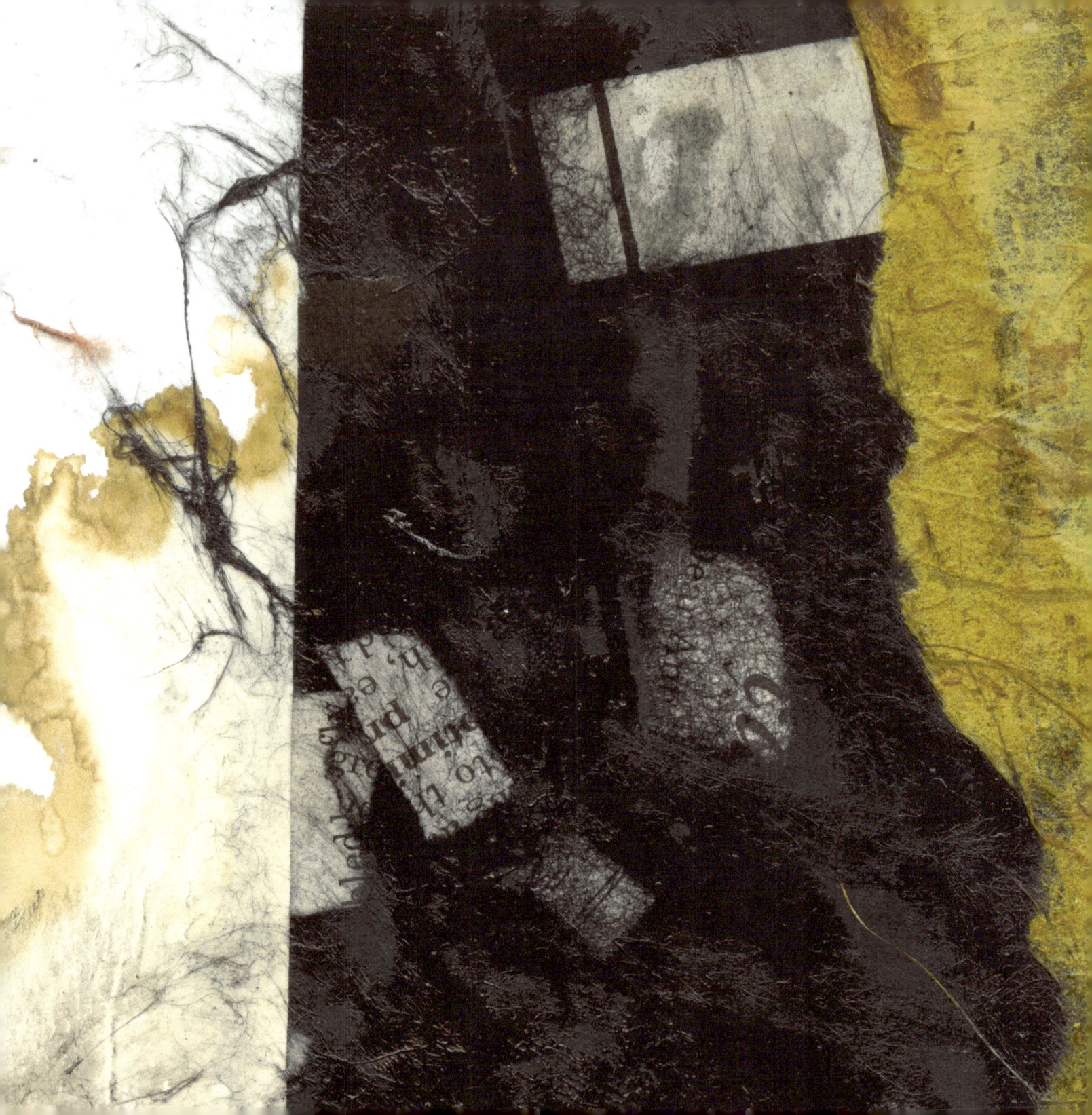

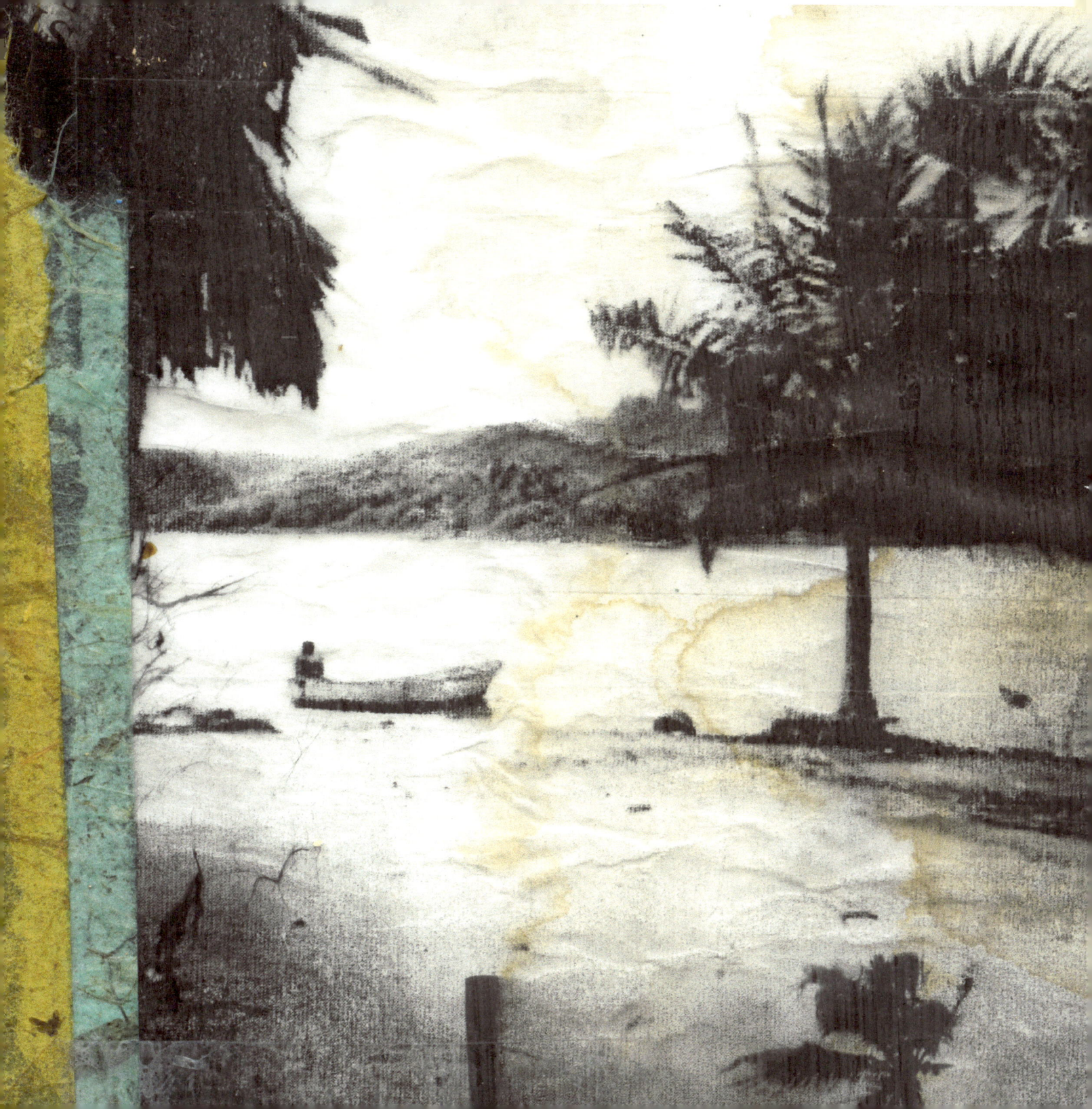

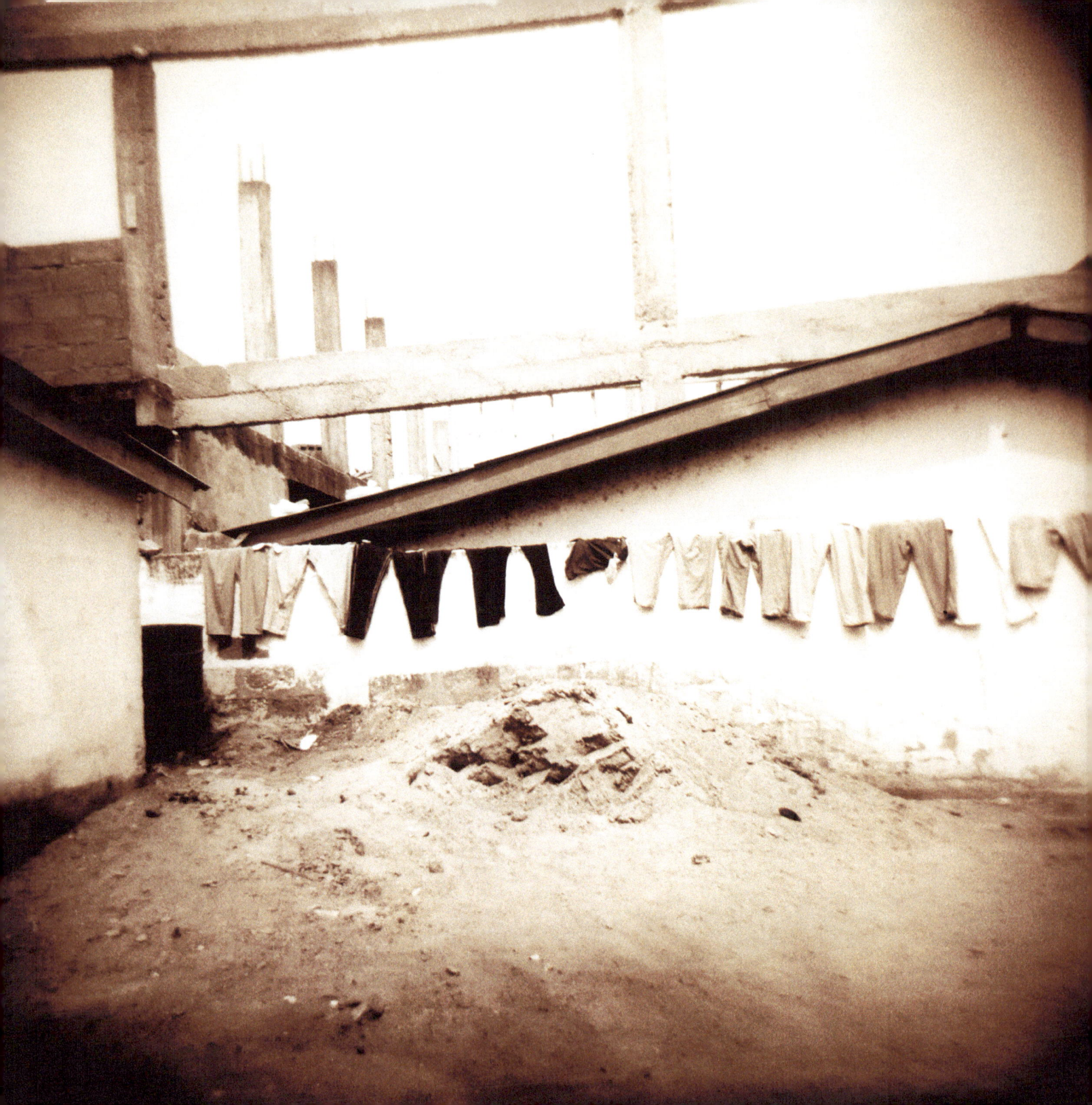

the rain parade

A Photographic Journey Across Ghana

Words & Images by Julia Blaukopf

THE RAIN PARADE
A PHOTOGRAPHIC JOURNEY ACROSS GHANA
is published by
Abingdon Square Publishing Ltd.
463 West Street, Suite G122
New York, NY 10014 USA
www.abingdonsquarepublishing.com

Edited by Nancy Wielunski

Designed by Ann Koivunen

Portrait of author by Rita Bernstein
www.ritabernstein.com

ISBN: 978-0-9830762-1-6
Library of Congress Control Number: 2011927281

Printed in the United States of America

table of contents

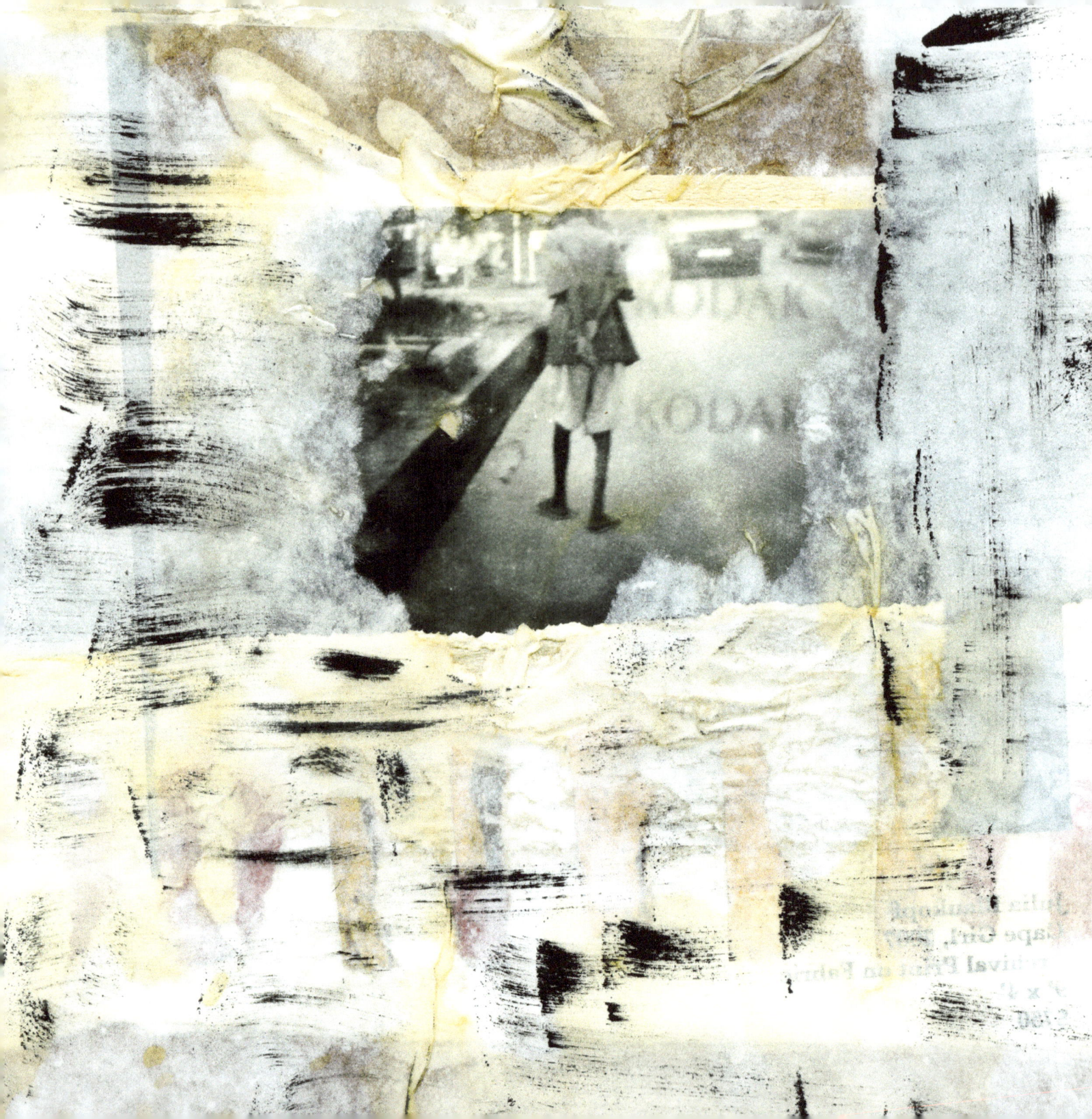

WOVEN INTO THIS
BOOK ARE MY GLIMPSES
OF THE EVERYDAY, OF
MOTHERS, ARTISANS,
LEADERS, WORKERS,
AND WOMEN WHO
USE IMAGINATION TO
ACHIEVE PROSPERITY
FOR THEIR FAMILIES
AND THEIR COUNTRY.

Foreword

2006, I am in Accra, Ghana. Over the next four months I will work with Women in Progress, an organization that empowers women through a sustainable business of clothing production called Global Mamas.

The two co-directors, Renae Adam and Kristin Johnson invited me to live in Cape Coast and work with them as a photographer. Renae established the Global Mamas office and storefront along with a thriving volunteer program and home in the city of Cape Coast. I will soon live in what Renae says is a very comfortable home just across the street from a large hotel in Elmina. Renae is my role model. She and Kristin, who is based in the US, work tirelessly.

During the four months I lived in Ghana I traveled throughout the country visiting the bead-making region, mountain villages, seaside retreats, a remote fishing village, the big city of Accra, and the homes of Ghanaian artisans and professionals. I scribed my experiences into a journal, detailing the overwhelming details of each day.

These written impressions interact with the photographs to create my story – a time that becomes a dream.

The characters in my tale consist of Ghanaian artisans working with Global Mamas and volunteers who are presented in a stream of momentary encounters. Woven into this book are my glimpses of the everyday, of mothers, artisans, leaders, workers, and women who use imagination to achieve prosperity for their families and their country.

These images were first exhibited at the 2007 First Person Arts Festival in Philadelphia. Entitled *The Ghana Tales*, this exhibit promoted the mission of Women in Progress and told the stories of Ghanaian women, some of which are captured in these pages.

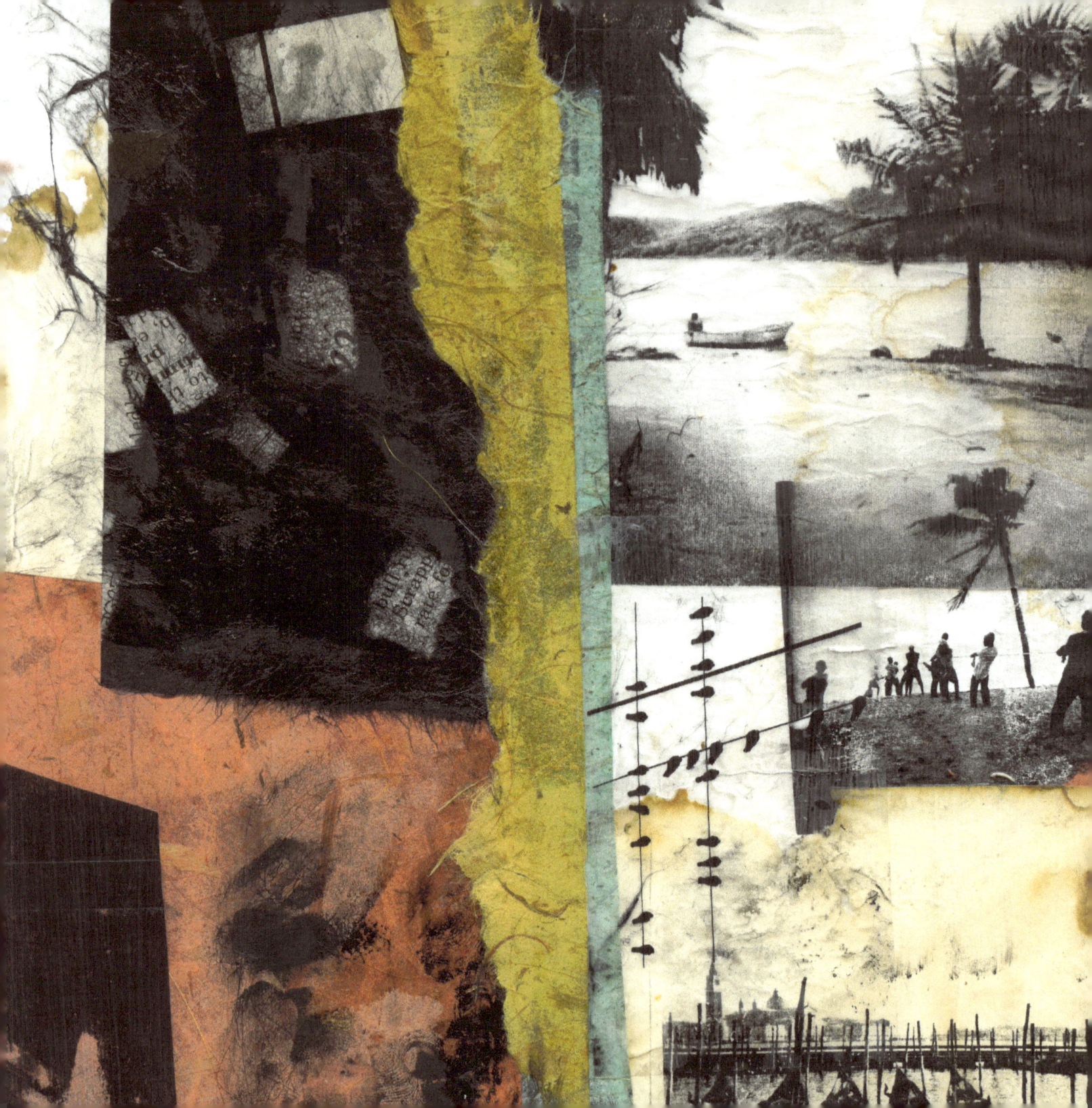

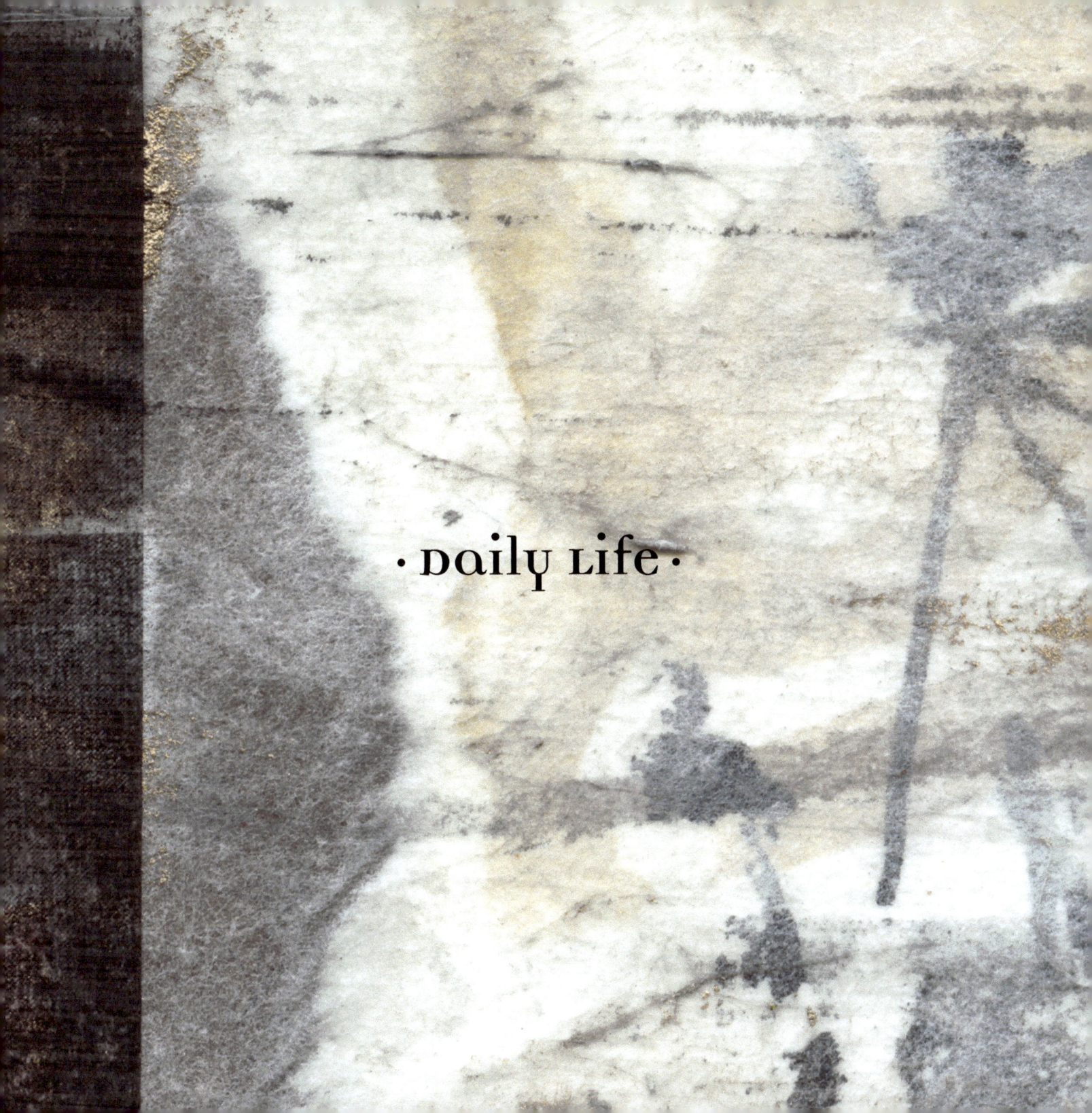

· daily life ·

Sleeping to Crickets and Waking to Roosters

THE SMELL OF SMOKE SPREADS ACROSS THE THICK, MUSTY AIR. JUST OUTSIDE OF THE AIRPORT LIES TIMES SQUARE, GHANA STYLE.

Bright billboards, loud bars, and restaurants featuring food from Chinese to Lebanese fare spread across several blocks. Mandy, Renae's one American employee at Global Mamas, offers me a plastic bag filled with filtered water. I bite the corner off and suck the warm water out from the end. Renae drives us to a large house where she rents "the boys quarters". The place consists of two rooms, a living room and a washing room, plus a toilet space. Women in Progress volunteers use this small apartment when visiting Accra. Outside the property's large gate, a man from the North sits patiently guarding the house. He celebrates Ramadan, and will only eat the leftovers Renae offers at night. Many Ghanaians have servants from the North since the pay is much better here.

Along the dirt road from Accra to Cape Coast, men and women mosey past cars, selling a variety of items that appear to float weightlessly on their heads. Women balance baskets of fruit and trays carrying gadgets. One man carries a large suitcase on his head, with two others in his hands. The figures wave around in the humid breeze.

The city is constantly bustling. Women roast fresh plantain along the street on top of hot coals. It is delicious. I am astounded that I can get coffee on the street in Ghana, never in Kenya. Of course it is instant Nescafe but still, it's better than nothing. A woman at a small bright blue kiosk sells tea, coffee, and egg sandwiches. I bring my own mug to her and she fills it with fresh Nescafe, and then places the cup in a black plastic bag. Everything eventually ends up in a plastic bag.

People carry unbelievable loads on their heads. Sellers of bananas, bread, bags of freshly cut pineapple mingle with others, crowned with even larger bowls of lettuce and tomatoes, fried plantains, bras, fresh fish, backpacks, and blocks of wood, just to name a few. Babies swing on their mothers' backs in colorful fabric. Little feet peek out in front from their mothers' sides. The smell of poop and foul car exhaust fills the dirt road. Thin gaps separate the road from the sidewalk. One wrong step could result in a three-foot fall toward a stream of water and garbage.

Occasionally the power goes out in the area. To conserve energy, the government shuts the electricity down in certain regions for an entire day.

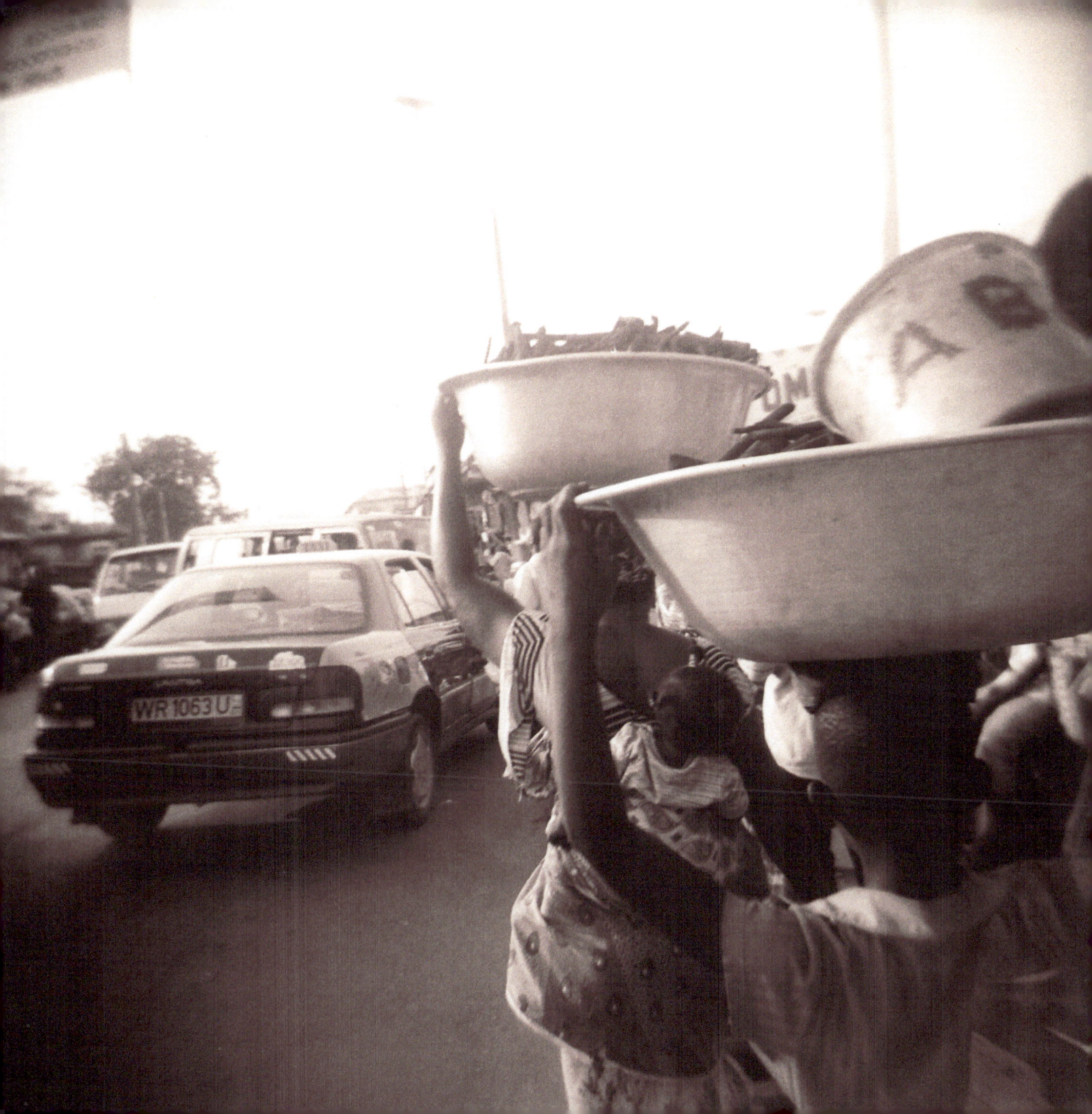

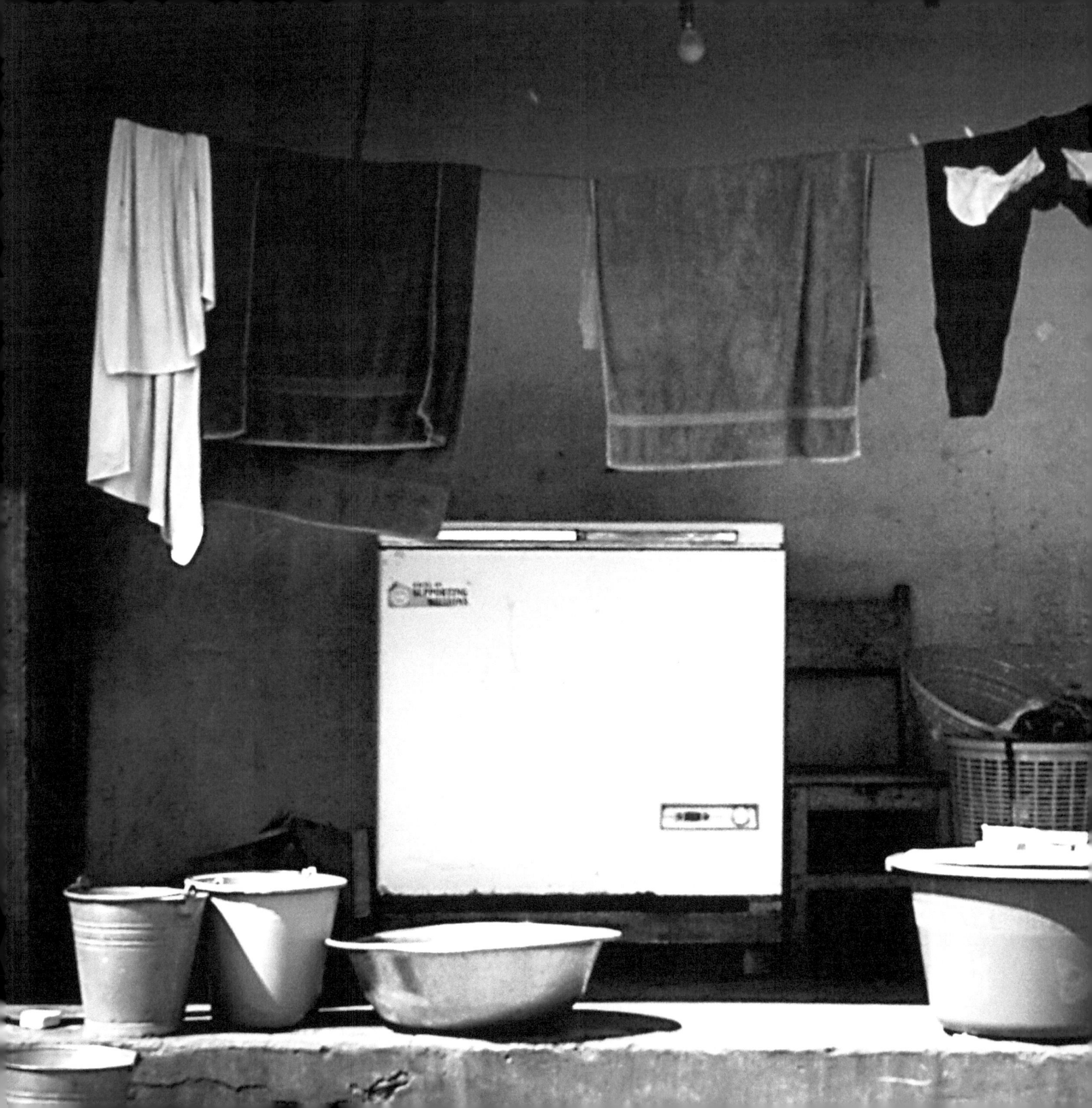

Language

People generally live in more remote areas. They come into the city to sell goods, like fish, fried food, yogurts, etc., and return to their village at the end of the day. Students, from very young to college age, live in hostels in the city.

Even though English is the official language in Ghana, most people converse in their tribal tongue. The language varies from one region to the next. English comes second. In the past, Renae had some odd problems with miscommunication. A former employee named Patience scrawled down notes during a store meeting. Renae suggested they mark wholesale goods in the store as reduced, regular, or bonus.

She noticed Patience's notes read, "Markdown goods as REDUCED, REGULAR and BONELESS."

EVEN THOUGH ENGLISH IS THE OFFICIAL LANGUAGE IN GHANA, MOST PEOPLE CONVERSE IN THEIR TRIBAL TONGUE.

Four in the morning, a man chants
in the distance…

hey-yaaaaah, hey-yaaaaaah, heyyaaaaaah…

To the west, a Muslim community
celebrates Eid-al-fitr, the last day of
Ramadan. Although the majority of
inhabitants are Christian, today is a
national holiday in Ghana.

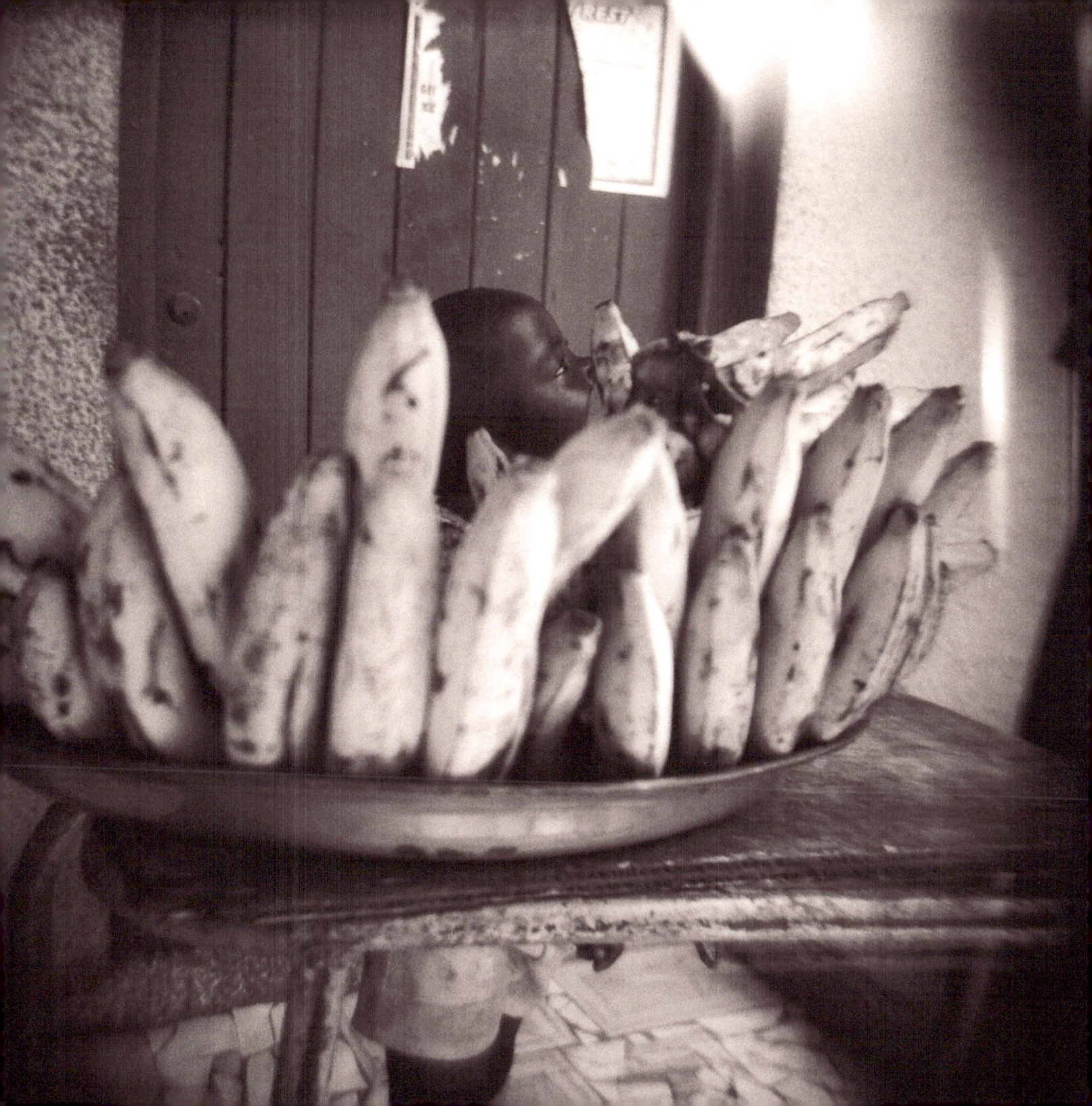

Lunch Break

The sounds of drumming compete with the pounding rain. Men and women in long linen robes of pink, yellow, and white dance down the street.

Up the way from a statue of a giant crab, bodies fill the market. Kiosks and wooden booths bump up against each other, one selling telephones, one oranges, the next a white refrigerator. Behind the kiosks lies a maze. Inside, a thin path spirals from one produce vendor to the next.

I swallow a nervous breath and walk farther in, hands starting to shake... "brunie, brunie," a woman yells to me from behind a booth of plantains. Her eyes are narrowed from the sun. I continue down, black olive eyes look up, offering their food, "what you want, what you want..."

Surprised faces appear behind endless tables of plantains, tomatoes, okra, and collards. "What are you looking for?" A woman touches my skin to "feel the white" as I pass.

14

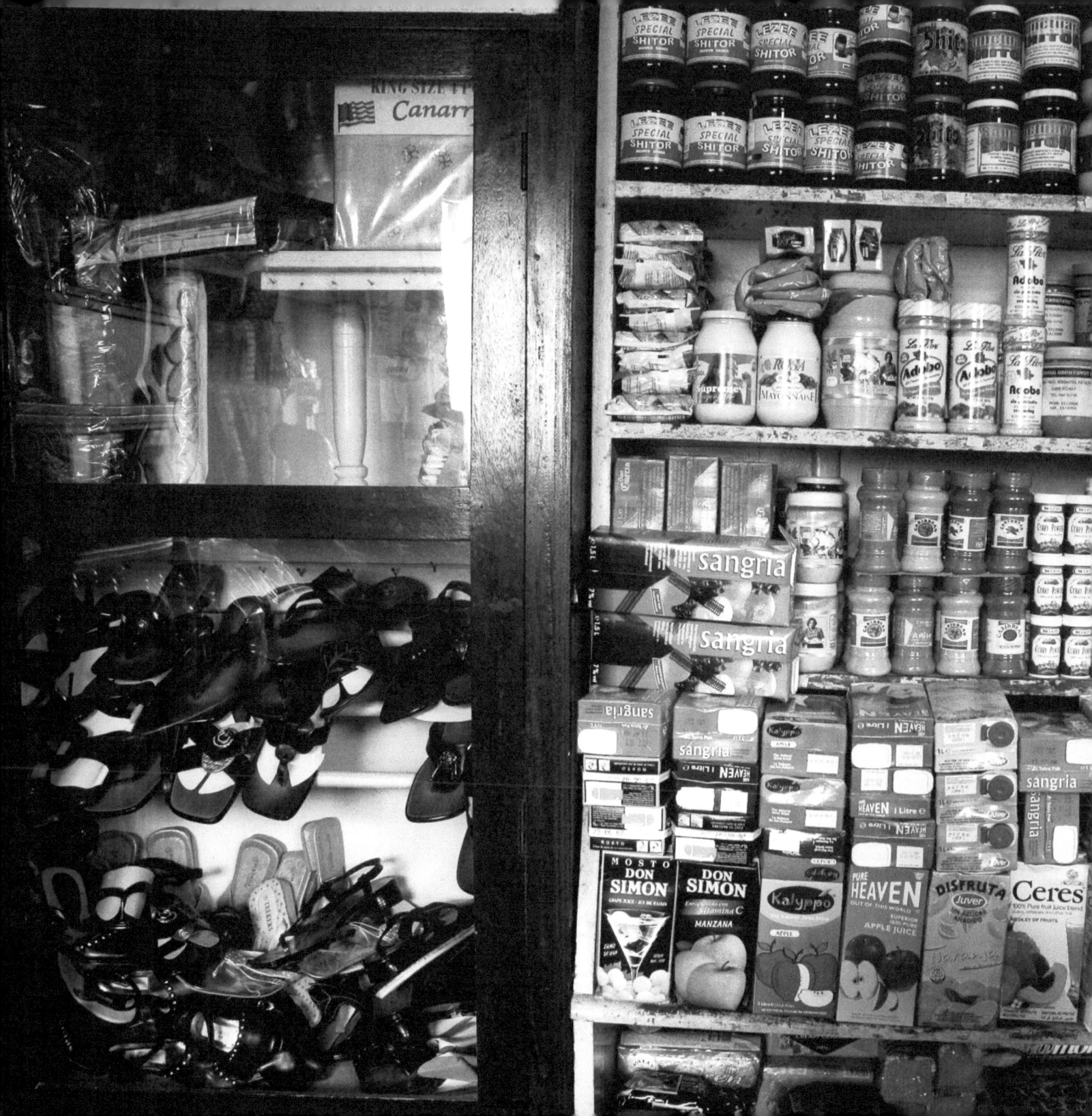

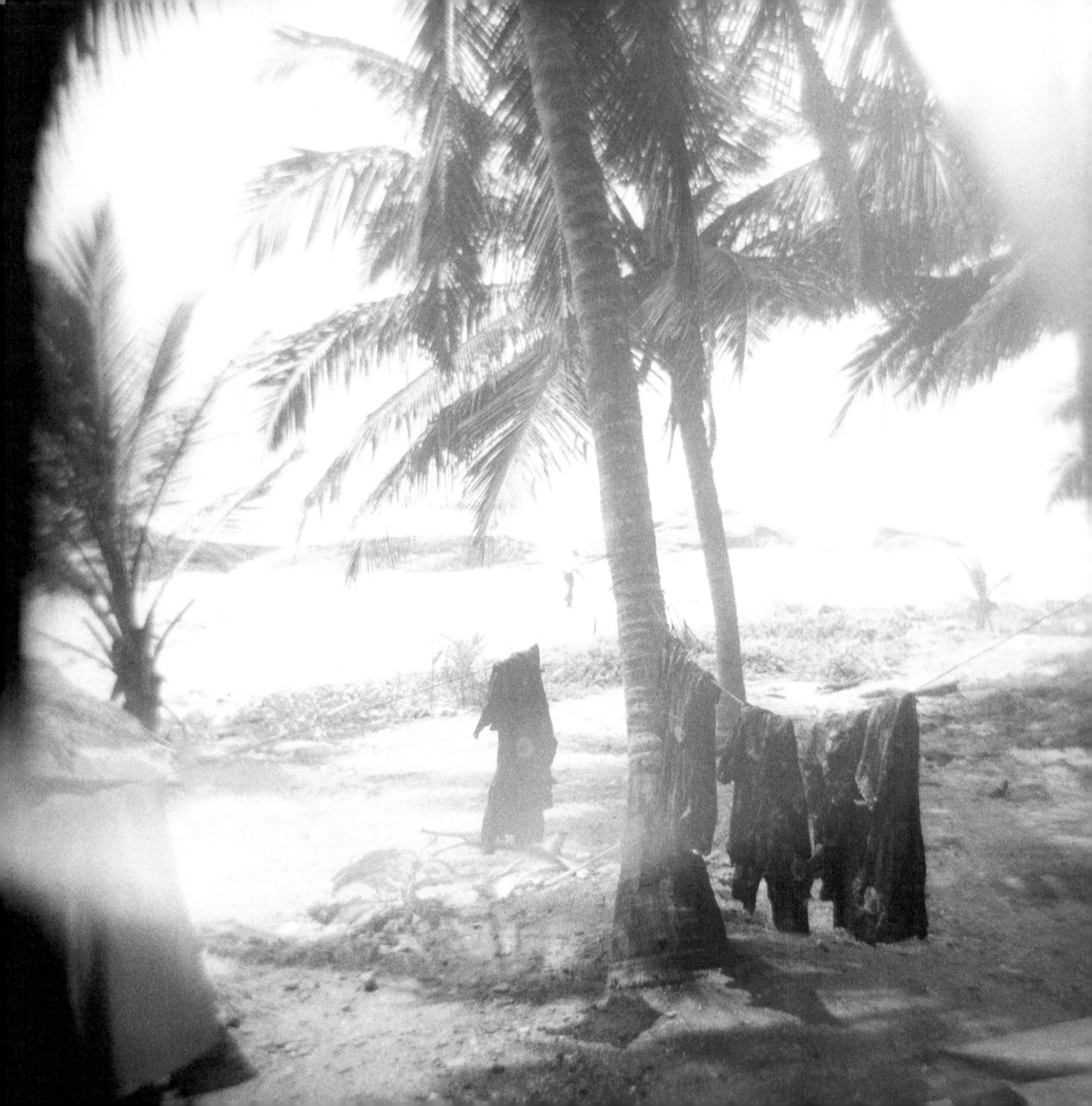

I am eating the best pineapple right now.
It was just rained on with cold water.

I can hear showers pounding down
outside the office.

The ceiling is weak. We have plastic
containers catching brown drips along
the wall.

Traveling to the Town of Ho

Miles before we reach Ho, a man boards
the tro tro carrying a long, lifeless antelope.
The carcass pokes out of a plastic bag.
Nicole unsuccessfully wills him away with
her eyes. He sits down next to her and slips
the cadaver at her feet. She looks ill.

Young women surround the tro tro at
the next intersection. They sell juicy
meat kabobs and slimy creatures. One
of the girls pats my hair while balancing
something covered in crumbs.

"You want? It is grass-cutter." Kabobs sit
like a popsicle-stick shack above her head.

"Grasshopper?" I ask.

"No! Grasscutter!"

"Ohhh, Grass-cutter – what is that?
Goat, cow, antelope?"

"Yes," the girl replies.

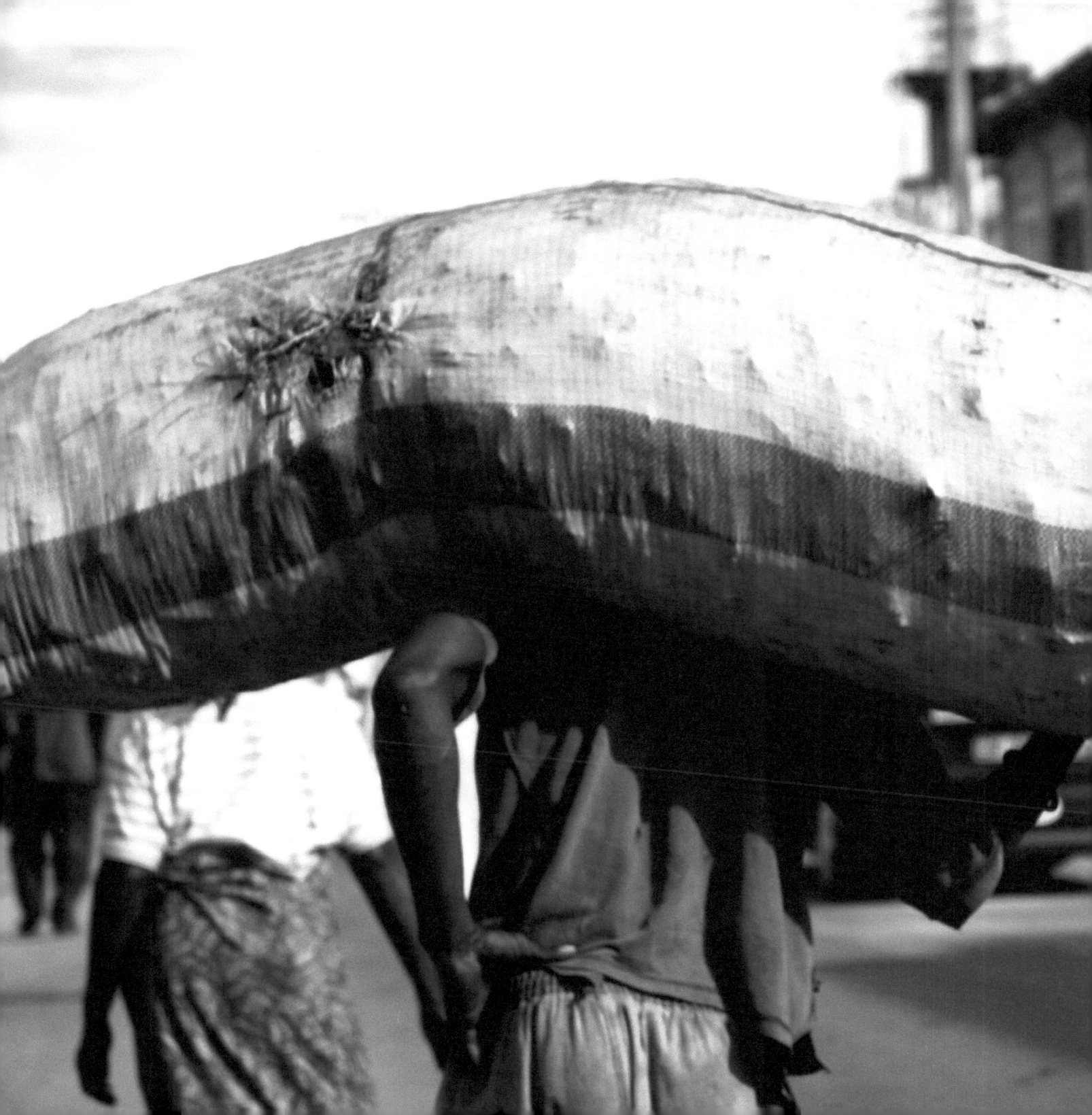

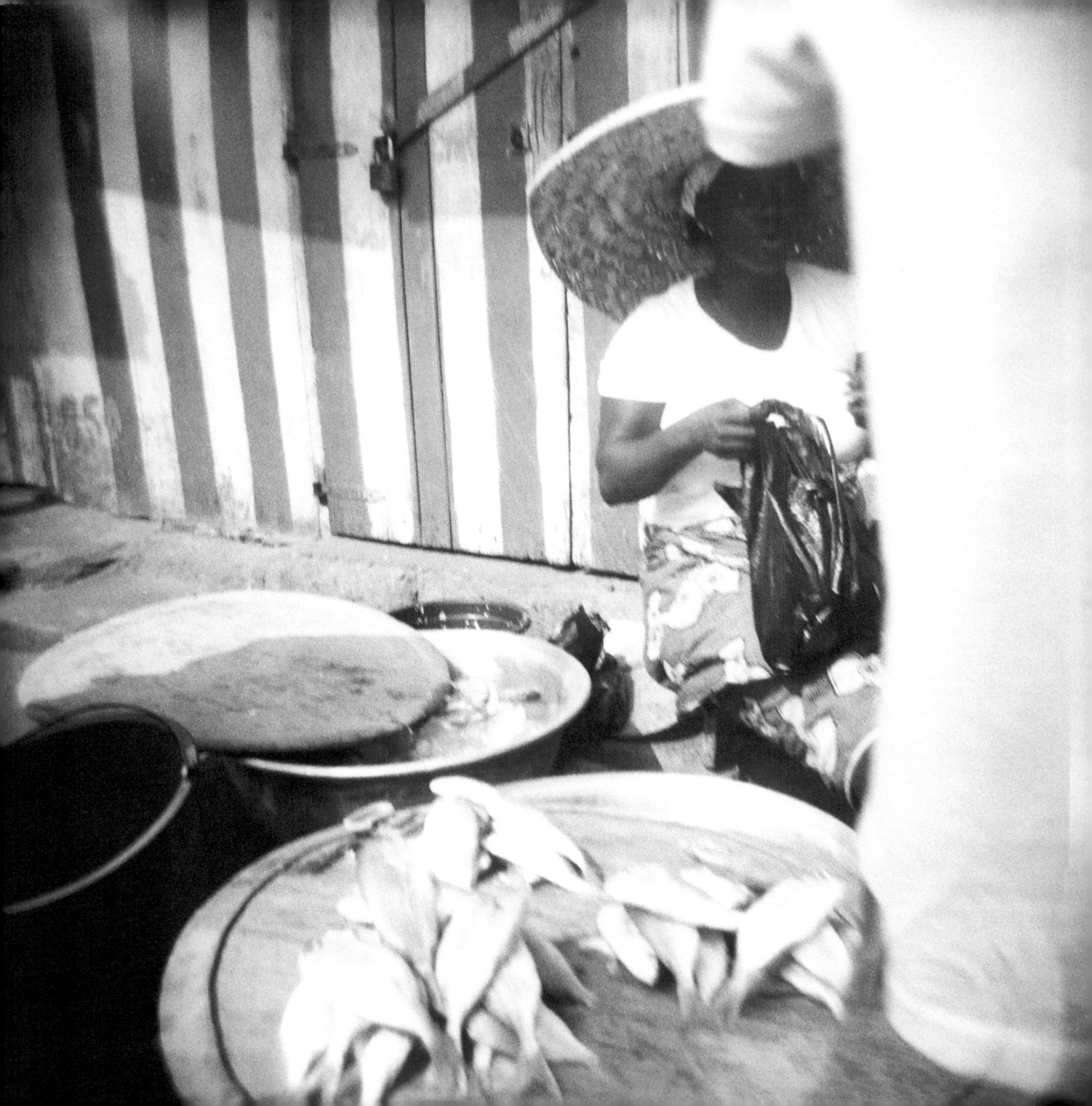

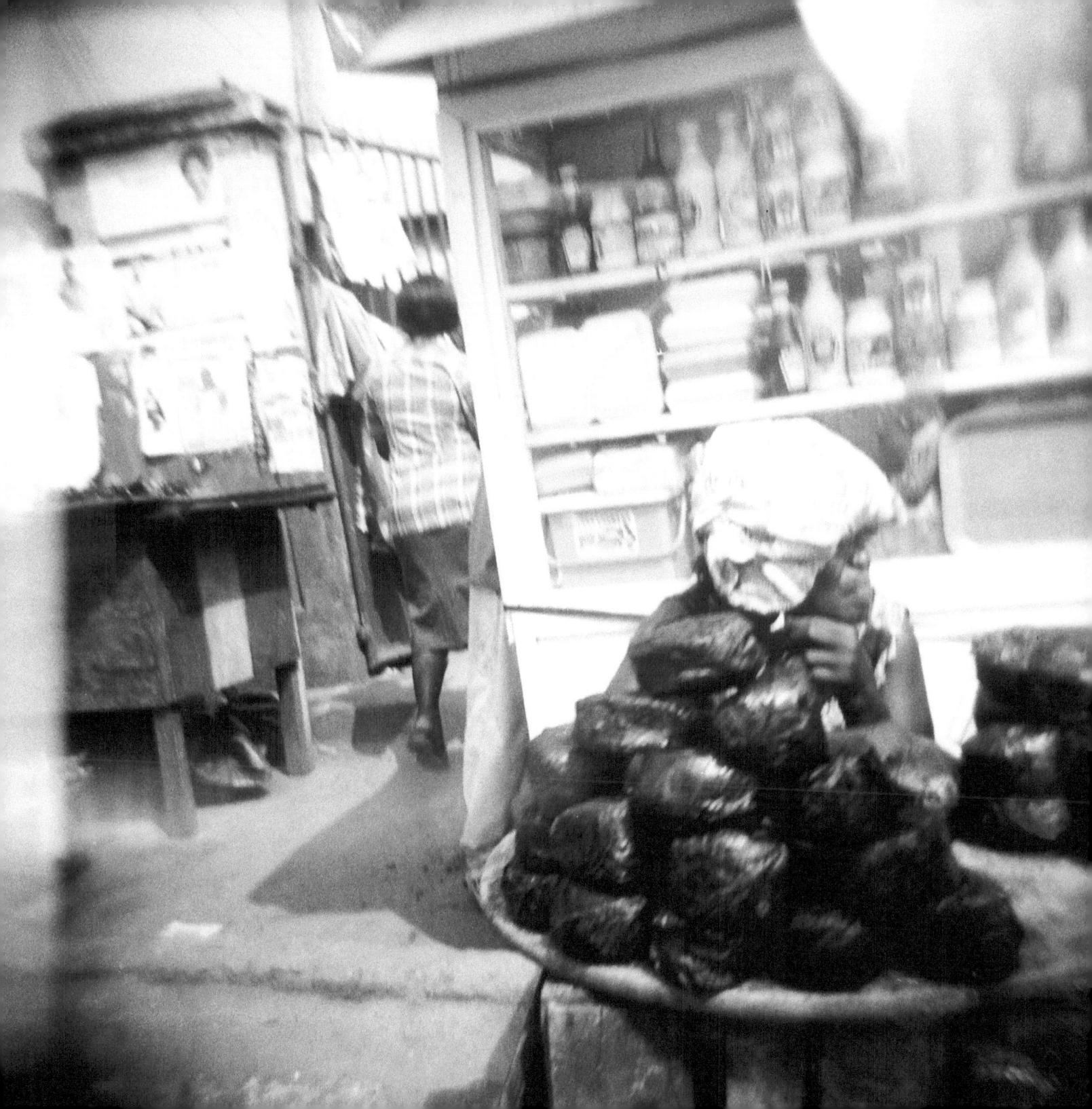

Wanderers

PEOPLE BELONG TO TRIBES, BUT IT IS NOT NECESSARILY AN INTEGRAL PART OF THEIR LIVES AS IT WAS YEARS AGO.

The tribes parallel religions in the cultural regard. The Ewe people comprise the smallest group in Ghana. Nonetheless, they hold the highest number of official positions, and place the most emphasis on education. Although the home base is in the Volta region, the Ewe people wander and disperse to pursue jobs, education, and so forth. They are the wanderers of Ghana. I live in a Fante tribal region; however, many of the fishing villages scattered throughout represent the Ewe people.

Many men wear long white, linen robes. There is a great influx of Muslims from the North. A fair sized Jewish community exists as well. Most people I meet are Catholic and Christian. Depictions of Christ appear on car windows, billboards, and even screensavers.

Renae says that Ghanaians love Jews. When a former volunteer mentioned to a batiker that she was Jewish, the woman smiled, hugged her, and pronounced, "You are the chosen one!"

I could get used to this.

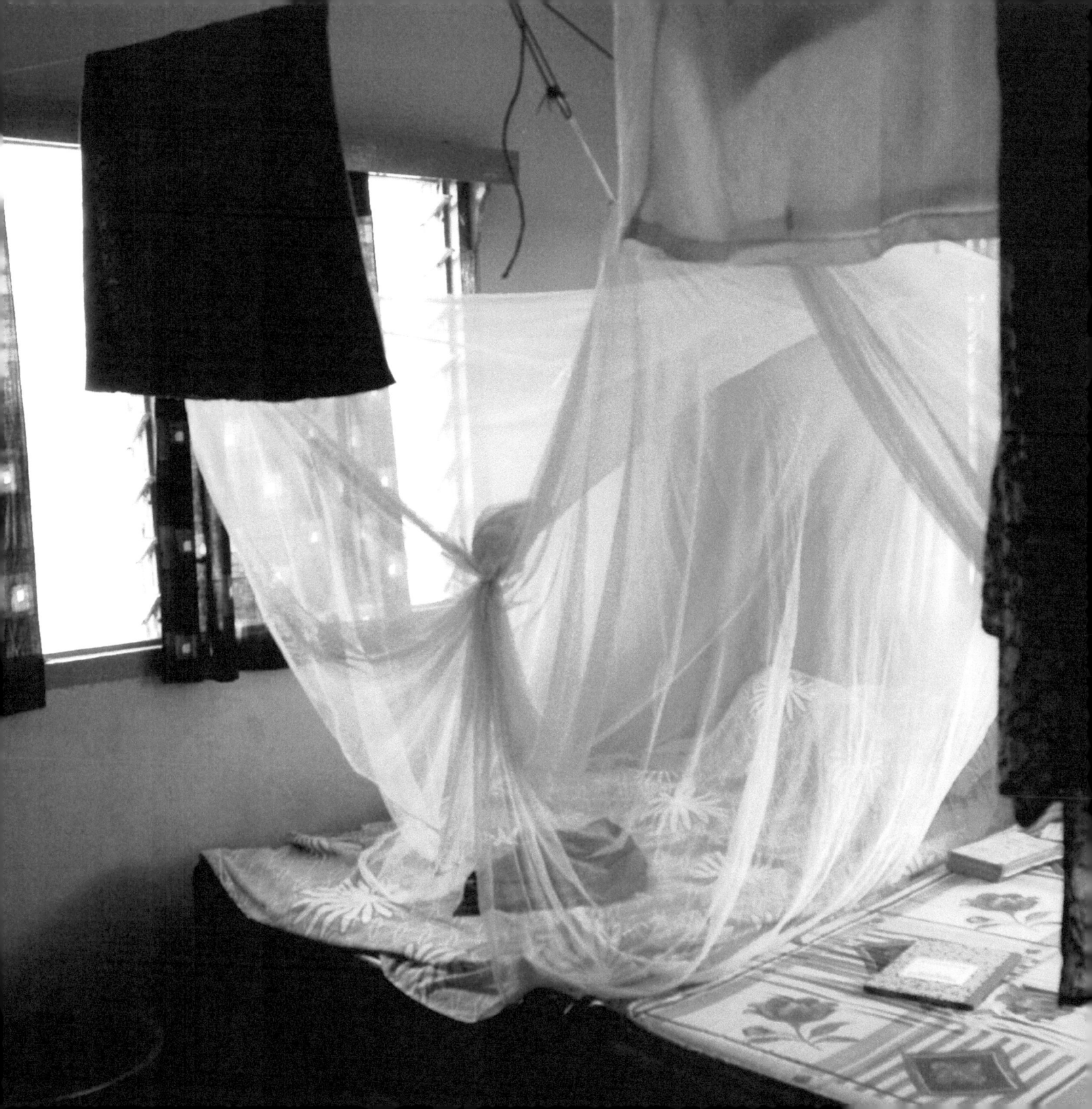

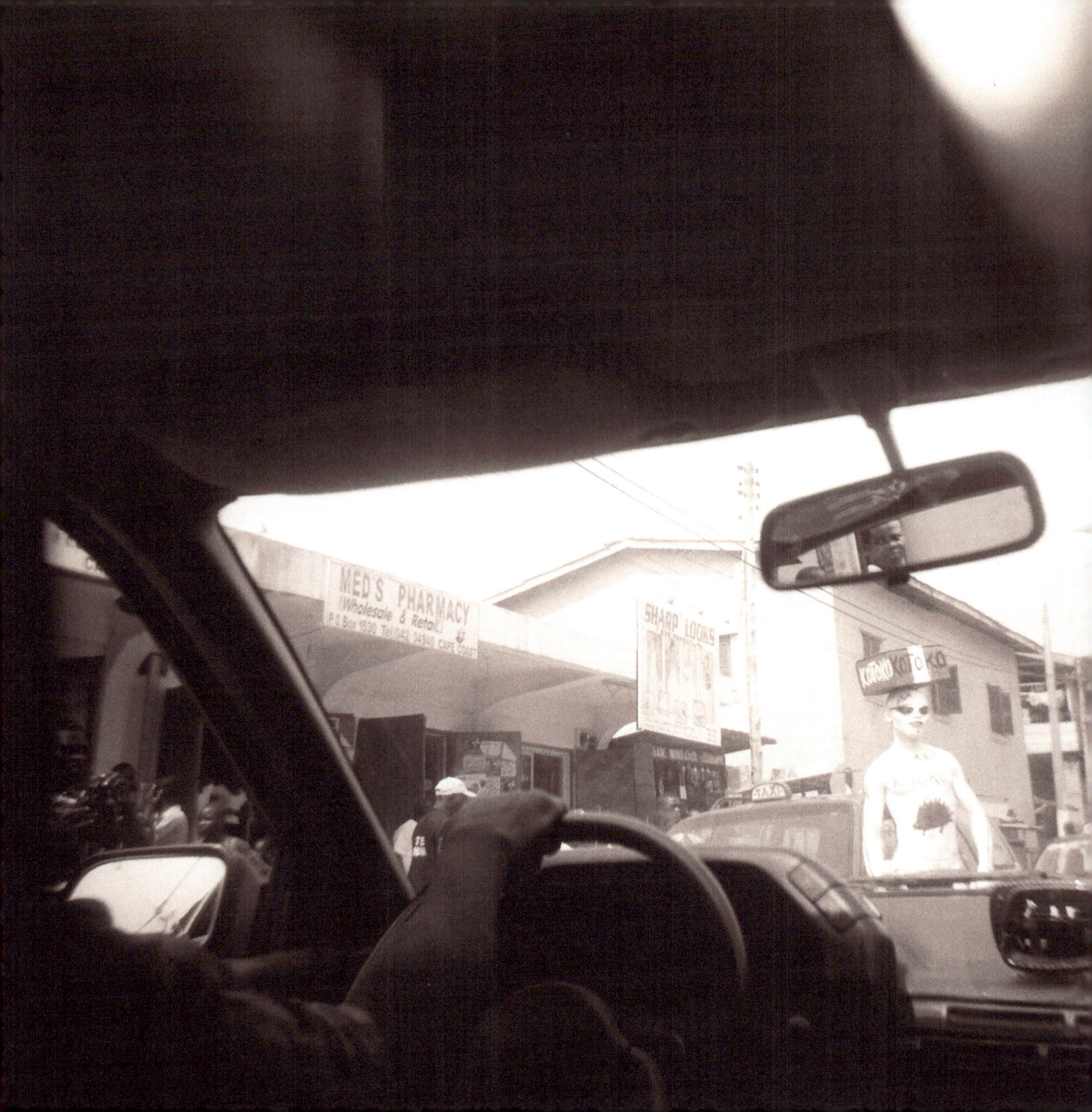

All Foreigners Are White

Ghanaians refer to African Americans as white, just as Europeans identify all Americans as Yankees. A foreigner in a car is a red flag for a money-bag. The cops will pull someone over and demand proof of every obscure law.

"Where is your first aid kit?!" A cop once demanded of Renae. She pulled a band-aid out of her backpack.

"Here!"

He found it acceptable.

25

Men are dressed in long white robes that
swing in the rain to the rhythm
of drums…

thump..thump..thump

High voices play behind the thumping
of rain drops…

hey-yaaa, hey-yaa, hey-yaaa

A parade runs down Kingsway, the main
thruway in front of the Global Mamas
store. Small children in frilly dresses chase
after the crowd. The sounds of drumming
compete with the pounding rain.

Men and women in long linen robes
of pink, yellow, and white dance down
the street.

I listen to drumming, singing, and shrieks
from beneath the ghostly veil of my
mosquito net.

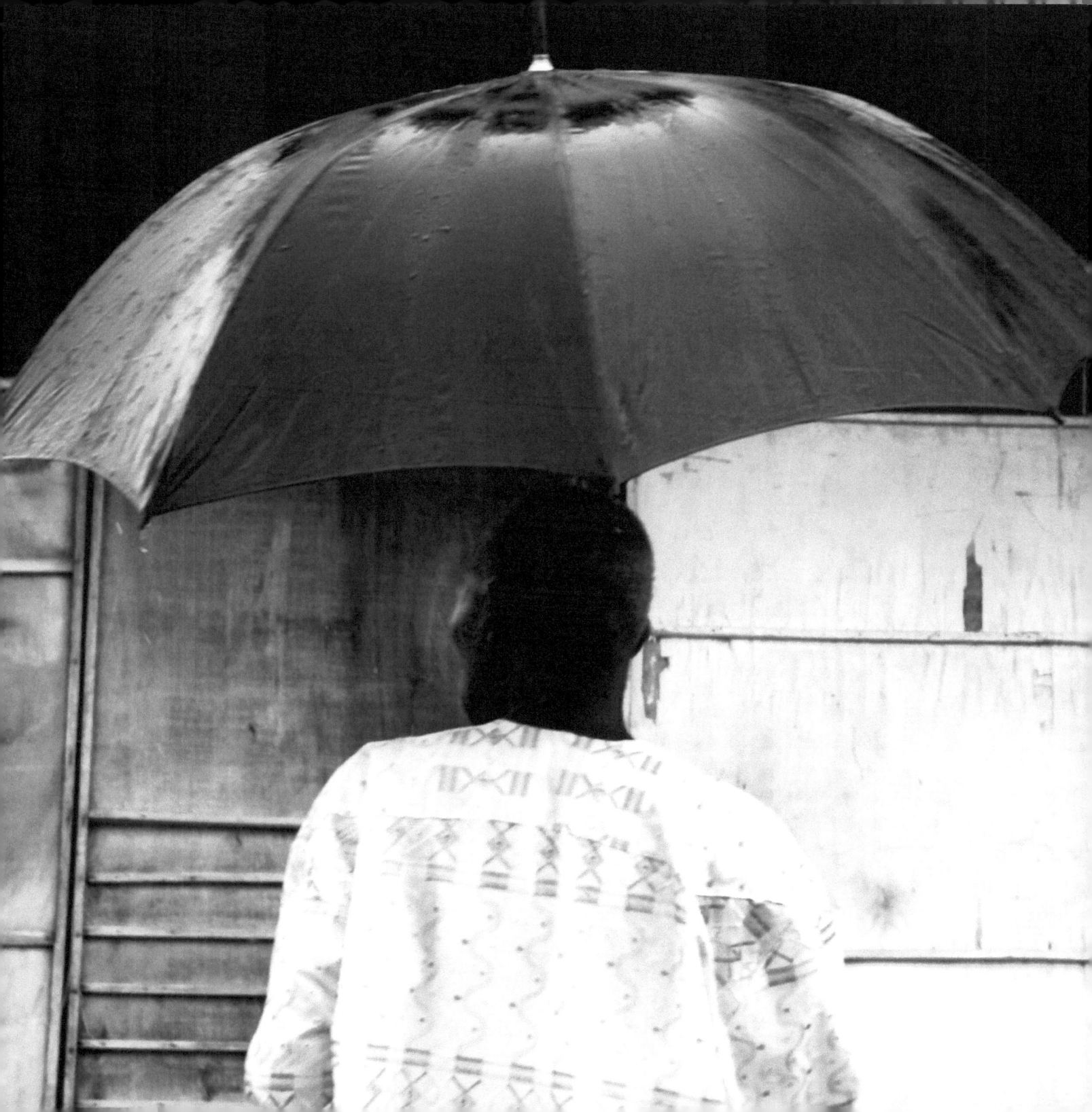

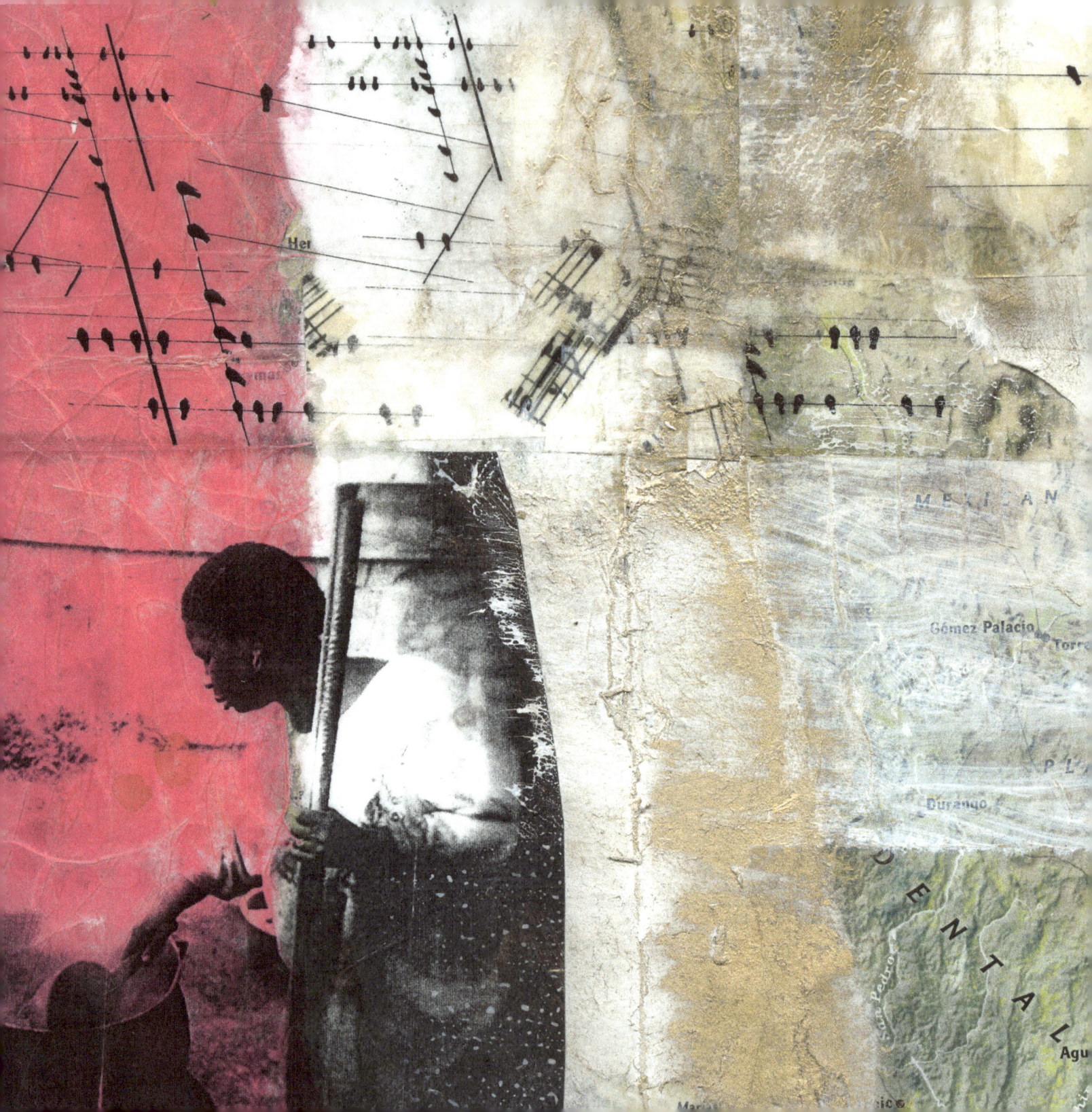

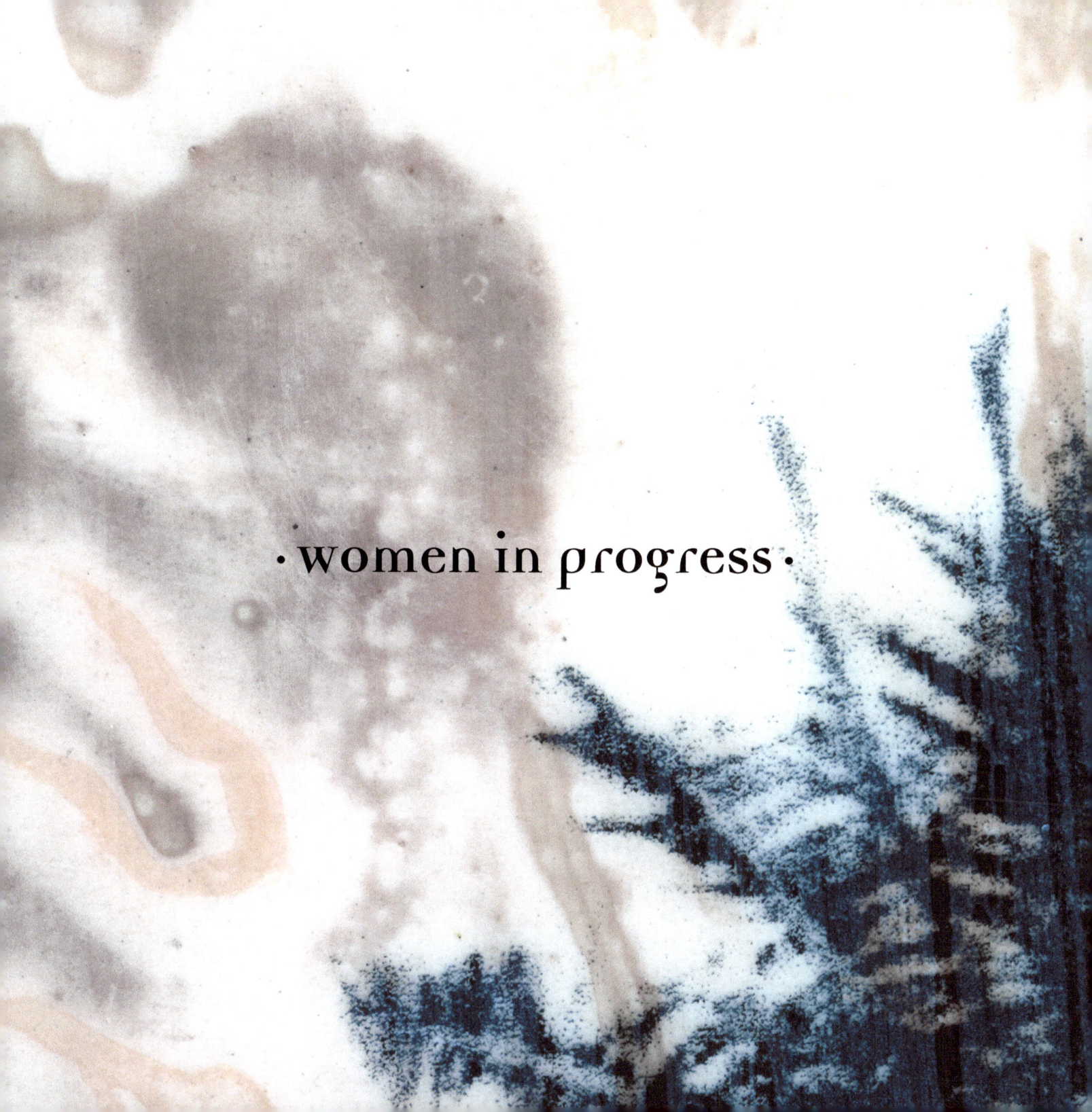

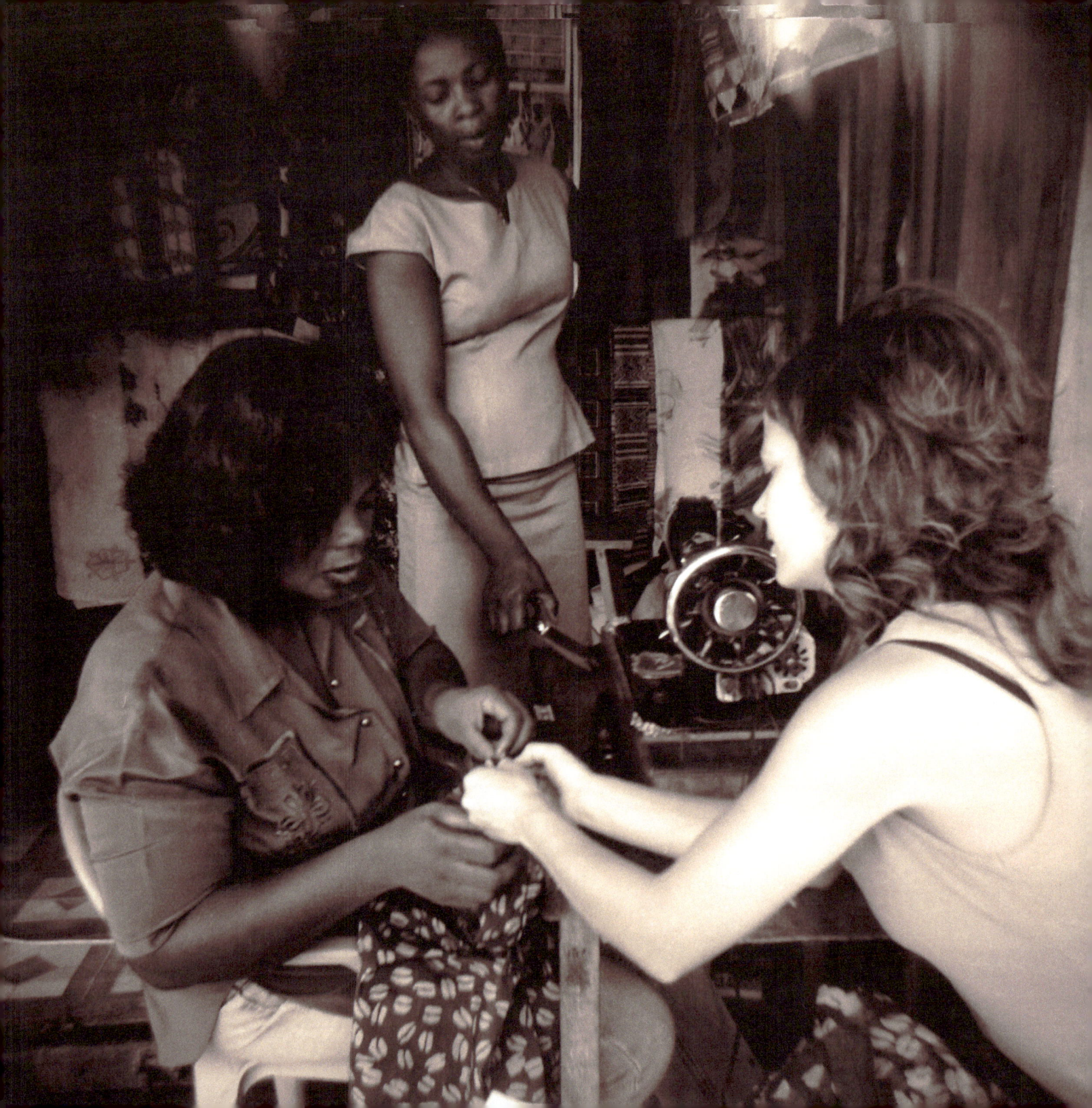

Sea Water Fish Fries...
A Base for Okra Stew

Agnes sits beside my makeshift set as I photograph a seemingly endless pile of garments for the catalog.

"Agnes, this is never-ending! Global Mamas has enough clothes. No more!"

"Julia, this is what you do, you are a photographer!"

"I don't like taking these kinds of photos."

"What kind of photos do you take? I notice everyone who comes here has a camera. Everyone who comes here takes photos. You cannot make much money in America when everyone takes photos, eh?"

"It's true Agnes. You should steal all their cameras."

"Oh Julia…when are you going to start photographing me? I am a woman of Women in Progress!"

"Give me time, I am here until January."

"Wow, why that long? Don't you miss home? Where is your boyfriend?"

"I don't have a boyfriend. You're supposed to find me one here."

"Julia, you can batik your shirt!" Agnes indicates my white tank top dotted with coffee stains.

"You don't like how I painted it in brown?"

"Why do you have so many coffee stains on your shirt?"

"I'm not good at aiming for my mouth Agnes."

"Yes, well you can batik that," Agnes reasserts.

"I know, but this is a shirt that I normally just wear around the house where nobody sees it," I lie.

"But you decided to wear it to work today."

The women in Ghana wear meticulous, well-kept dresses. New wigs emerge each week.

Volunteers arrive in tank tops, torn shorts, and bandanas wrapped around sweaty strands of hair. I have no explanation for wearing a visibly stained shirt to the office.

"I probably won't batik this. I do have a white skirt at the house with bigger coffee stains that I want to dye."

Agnes shakes her head in disbelief.

THE WOMEN IN GHANA WEAR METICULOUS, WELL-KEPT DRESSES. NEW WIGS EMERGE EACH WEEK.

Eli & Emma

Eli and Emma are two of the more successful batikers involved with Global Mamas. Their workshop is situated along the beach, about a forty minute walk outside the center of Cape Coast. The two women partner in the business that includes three apprentices. Emma has long black braids and an infectious smile.

When Renae approaches, Emma runs up from the beach with her arms open and grabs her in a tight hold. Eli saunters out with a more reserved smile. Since they became involved with Renae and Global Mamas, their business has started to thrive. They are now planning to buy a car, which is a huge deal in Ghana.

At noon, the two women rest inside their beachside workspace. Young apprentices melt the wax for the morning's work in iron cauldrons. A bird poops on my shoulder as Emma describes her second job as a volunteer nurses' assistant. She wears a brown badge shaped in a circle. Around the four sides read malaria, polio, AIDS, and another ailment. Malaria is as common as the flu here. Banners pronouncing "Malaria Walks to Promote Awareness of Prevention" string along the main road to Accra.

ELI AND EMMA ARE NOW THE PROTOTYPE OF SUCCESS FOR WOMEN IN PROGRESS.

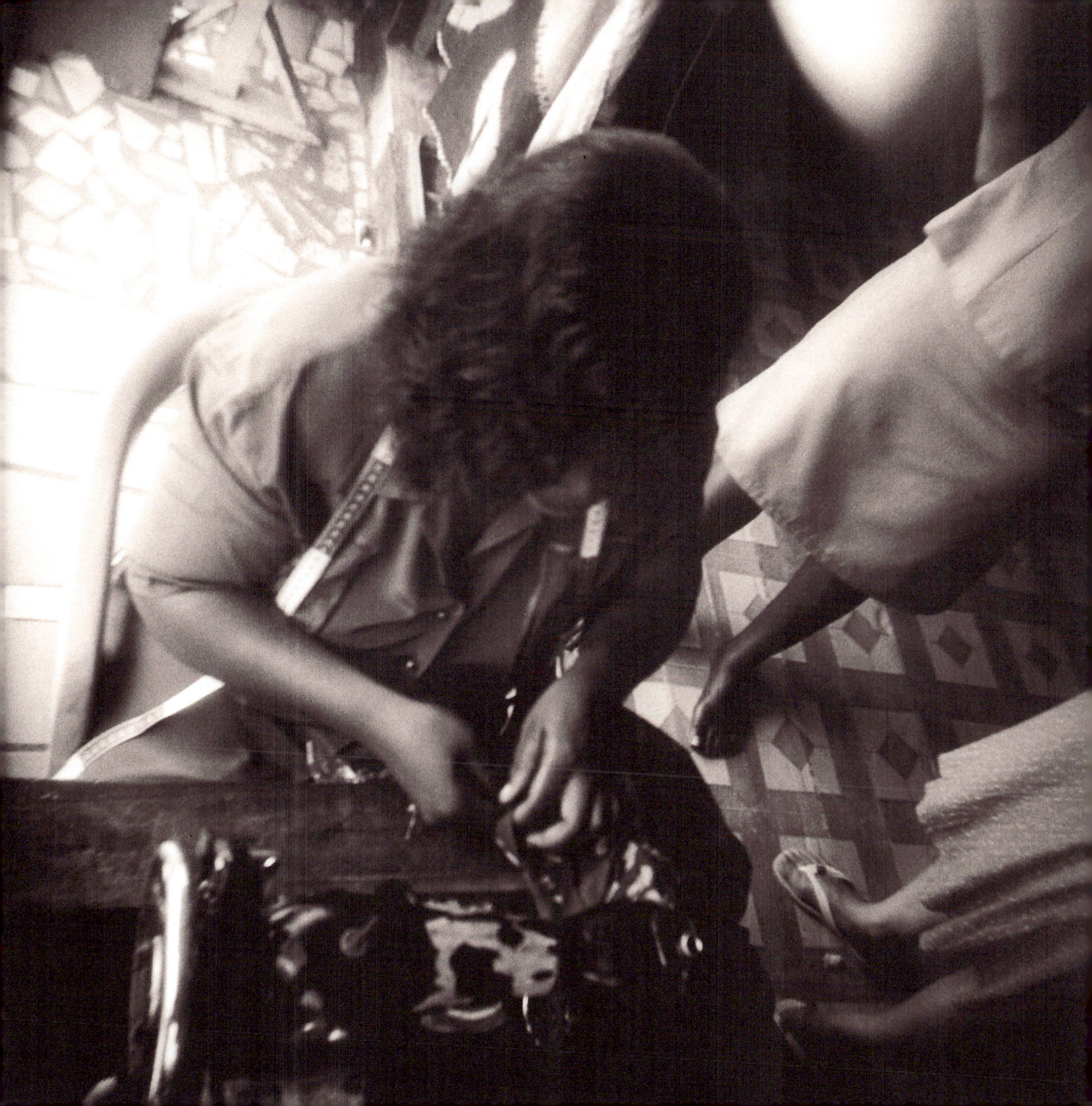

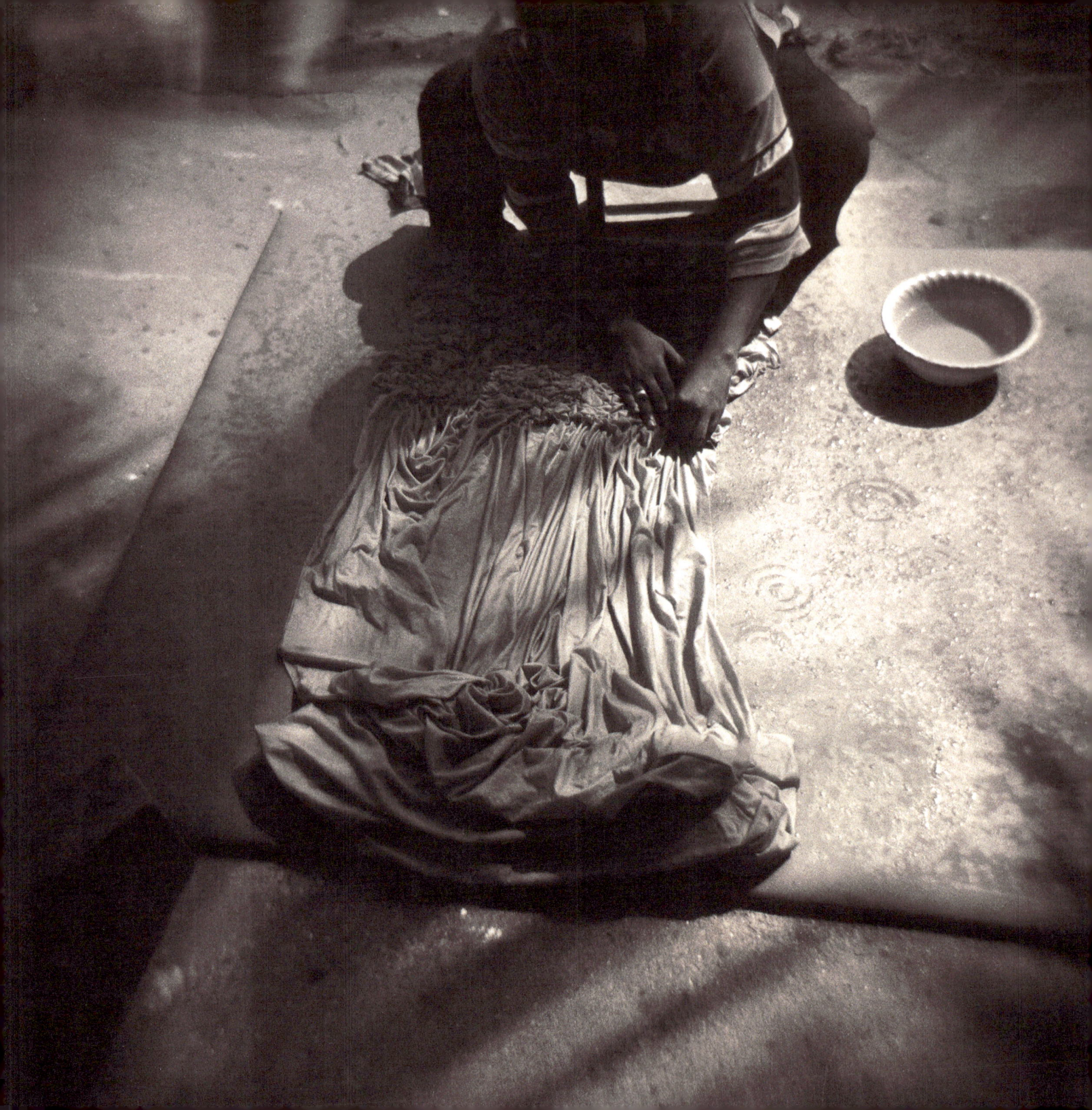

Women are trying on dresses printed
in polka dots.

Renae can't determine which items are
actually sized small, medium, or large.
Size determinatives are so different here.

Ghanians don't use numbers. Most women
make their own clothes. In the market,
one woman swears she is a medium, but
in U.S. standards, she is a large. The chart
says she is "almost a large".

In Paris she would be an XXL.

Gifty

SHE WORKS ALONE OUTSIDE, DYEING FABRICS BLOOD RED IN A SMOKY CAULDRON. WHITE FABRIC IS WOUND AROUND HER HAIR.

Another very successful batiker, Gifty, lives farther outside the city, on a hill overlooking crooked roads and double-decker pink apartments. She works alone outside, dyeing fabrics blood red in a smoky cauldron. White fabric is wound around her hair. Her two apprentices have just quit; they could not handle the pressure of the workload. Alone, she struggles to finish the work for the afternoon deadline. She approaches the cauldron and folds pieces of clothing over another one using two long poles. Then, she lays the cloth down on a wax-covered table beside rubber gloves, plastic spoons, and a deep blue plastic bowl.

The next workshop is much less grandiose. Mavis works with one apprentice in a small stone room. Her space is located behind a row of buildings, in a courtyard surrounded by broken walls, rubble, and lines of laundry. Next door, an enormous woman washes clothes in a bowl full of suds. Adjacent to underwear and onesies, a baby blue cloth hangs with sticky stamps of wax.

Normally well dressed and pleasant, Mavis looks weary in a dirty blue polo shirt and brilliant green mesh pants. Her hair extends to the side in stiff clumps. She mumbles to Matilda in soft-spoken Fante, their tribal language. Matilda turns to us and asks if we want to see her work.

A thick piece of wax shipped from Germany melts in an iron wok. Mavis waves the small fire brewing beneath to speed the melting process. We stand awkwardly in the tiny room. Eventually the block dissolves into a waxy liquid. She dips a foam stamp of a star into the wax and proceeds to mark white linen along preset lines. She continues for a few minutes before facing Matilda to ask if we have seen enough.

36

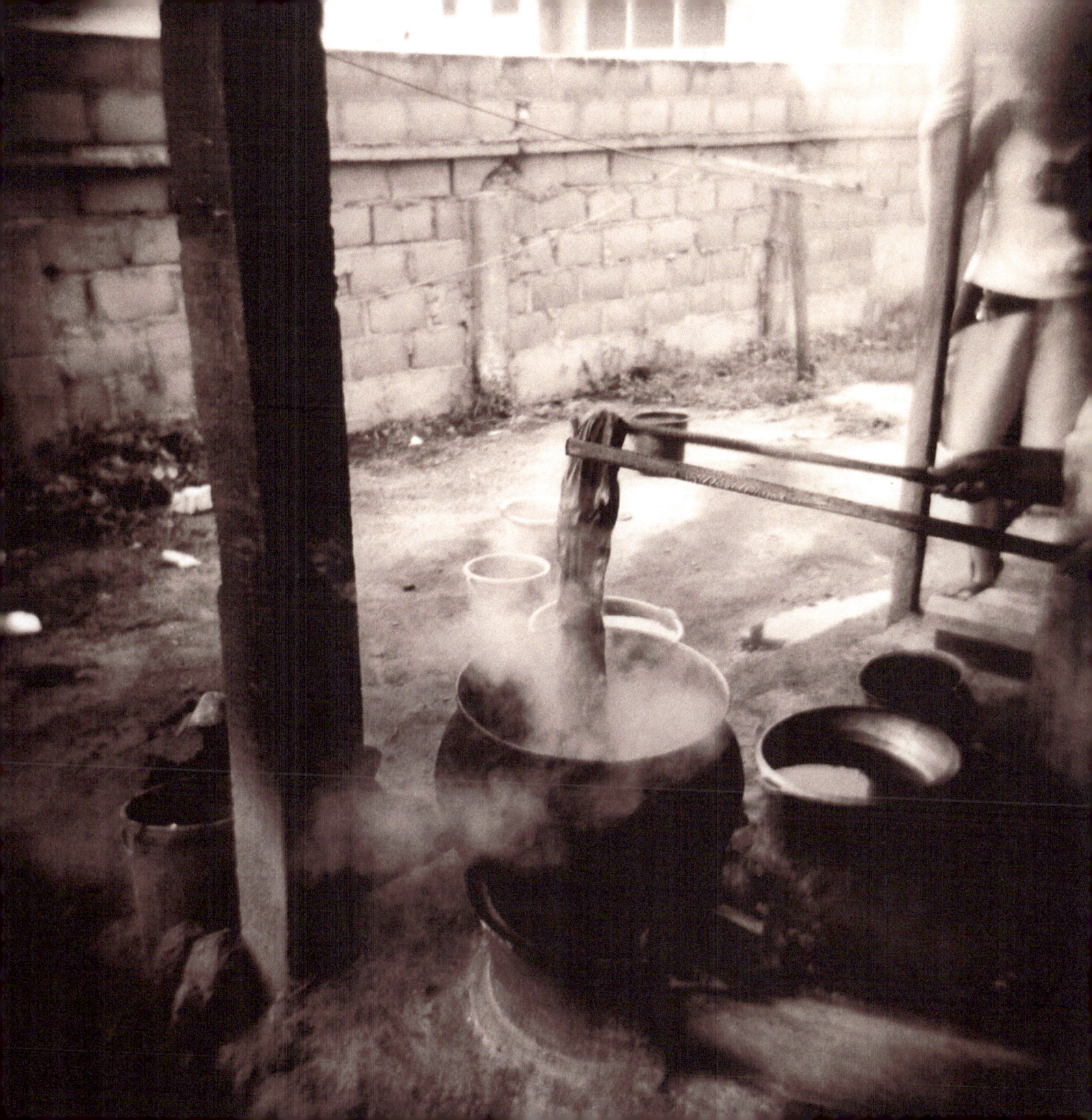

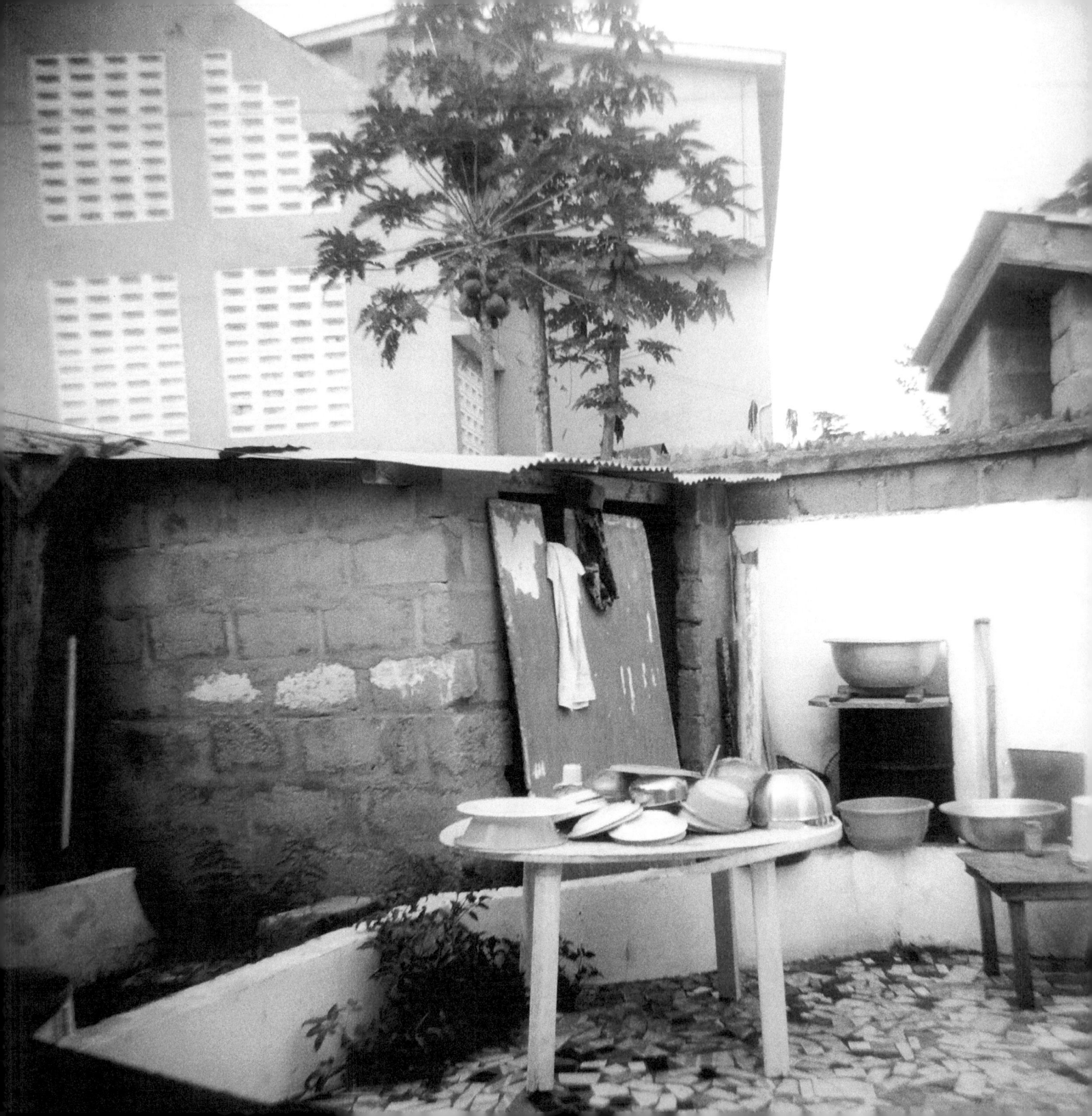

Police Raid

THE PINEAPPLE LADY RUNS AFTER THE MEN AS THEY SMASH HER TABLE. CHILDREN RUN PAST THE STORE SCREAMING.

We stop at two seamstresses' studios before taking a taxi back to the office. Traffic is backed up down the roads stemming from Kingsway. Dorkus directs the driver around the block to avoid the backup along the main road in town. Vehicles continue to pile up along the side route. People riot down the street. The taxi driver looks annoyed at us for directing him into the commotion. We scramble out of the car.

The chaos heightens as I near the row of pineapple vendors. Where wooden tables holding buckets of sliced fruit stood earlier, it is suddenly empty. An animated woman working at one of the pineapple stations yells toward the mass of people. Her deep red complexion is weathered and whiskered. Tears and perspiration paint her vicious expression.

Policemen in purple jumpsuits destroy one sidewalk store after another. They punch holes in each sign, including Global Mamas. The pineapple lady runs after the men as they smash her table. Children run past the store screaming.

It is illegal to sell on the street. The government gives the sidewalk shops one day's notice. If they do not leave, the police destroy their spots. This is the first time the police have actually ransacked businesses in Cape Coast. In Accra, it happens at least twice a month.

Teresa and Agnes sit beneath a pile of white fabric inside the front room. They explain the situation matter-of-factly, and then continue to work as if the chaos were a strand in everyday life.

39

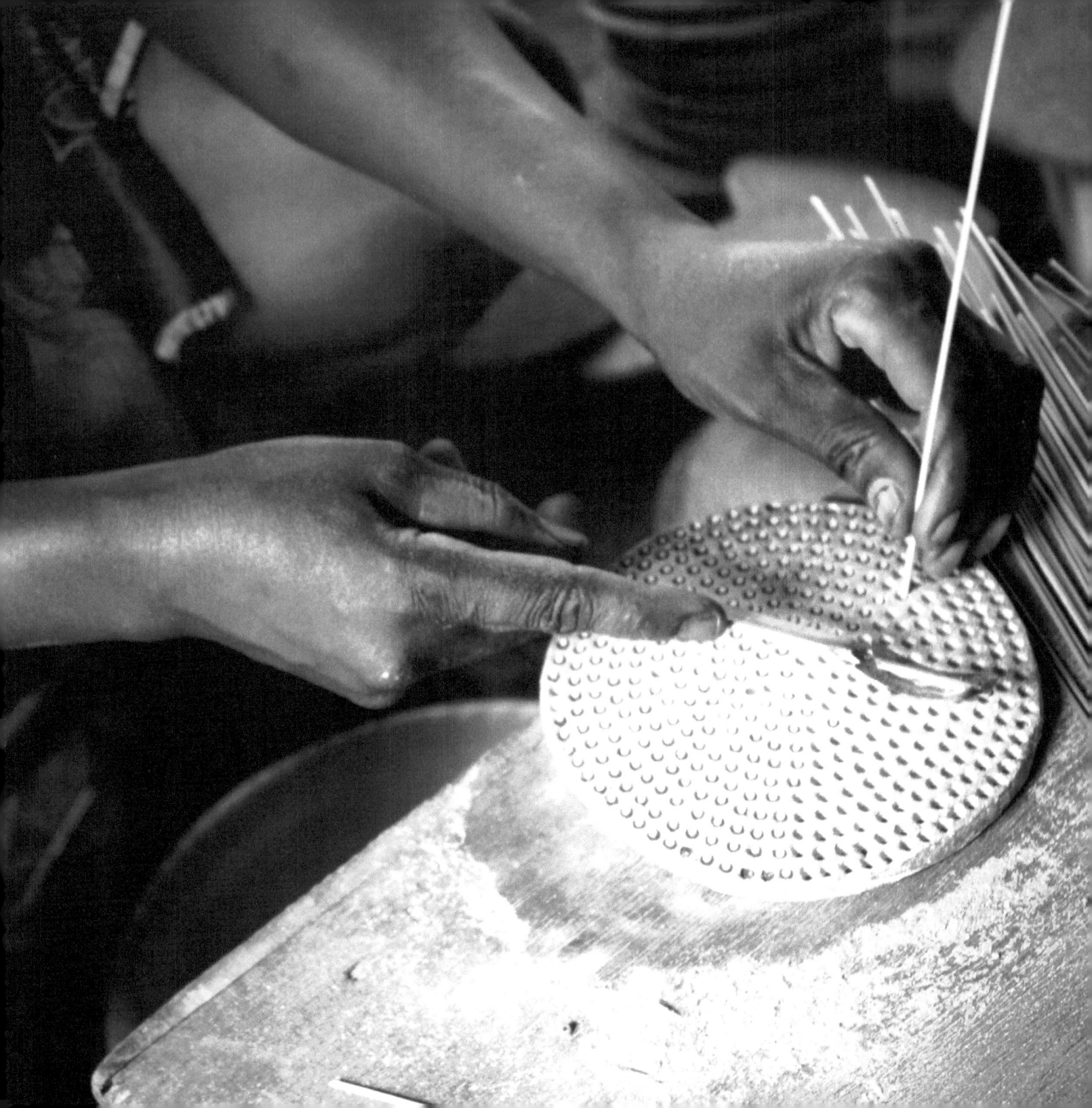

Beadmaking in Krobo

The office consists of two crammed rooms painted bright blue. White flowers applied with messy sponge brushes dance around the walls. Concrete floors are crowded with boxes, baskets of beads, and plastic furniture. Tables line the front room.

Tupperware containers sit in rows, holding various styles of local beads. The back room serves as the home. A stove, hotpot, and broken refrigerator constitute the kitchen. Beside the kitchen sits a bed and four extra mattresses, leaning against the wall. A bare fluorescent lamp tints the room in green. An air conditioner hums vigorously. The back door leads to a communal courtyard. Laundry dries on the lines running above a jungle of buckets and chickens. A woman fries a sauce of hot peppers on a wood fire. Her son Isaac saunters around in checkered boxers.

Under the scorching sun, Elisha and I photograph new bead products for the catalog. Isaac approaches us curiously, peeping his head above our set. We kick away chickens that peck on our project. I flick ants between shots.

Toward night, the women reemerge to pound fufu, a soft dough eaten with soup or stew, in large wood bowls and fry yams for sale on the street.

To collect water for the house, Mandy pays local children with hard candy. The community shares two waste buckets enclosed in a wood stall as a bathroom. A makeshift wood seat covers the deep mess that continues to fill over two days. The odor is suffocating in the small space.

41

Comfort

She works beneath a tin awning in an amber-toned open courtyard. A shirtless boy watches her demo from next door. Using circular clay bases that resemble large coasters, she crafts the tiniest size of bead. To create the mold, she sticks thin green branches into the holes and slices the top off with a knife. She then sifts purple powder onto the base to stiffen and harden into glass. The powder bakes and hardens in a small wood oven for at least forty minutes.

Comfort smiles cheerily, answering occasional questions about the process in broken English. A neat scar protrudes from her triceps. She customarily takes the finished beads to the Global Mamas office in large plastic containers, instead of stringing them on thin lines, as she would for Cedi Beads. Stringing the beads for the market takes twice the time.

Comfort now works solely for Global Mamas since Renae pays twice as much as Cedi Beads.

ONE OF THE MORE RELIABLE BEAD ARTISANS INVOLVED WITH GLOBAL MAMAS IS A WOMAN NAMED COMFORT.

42

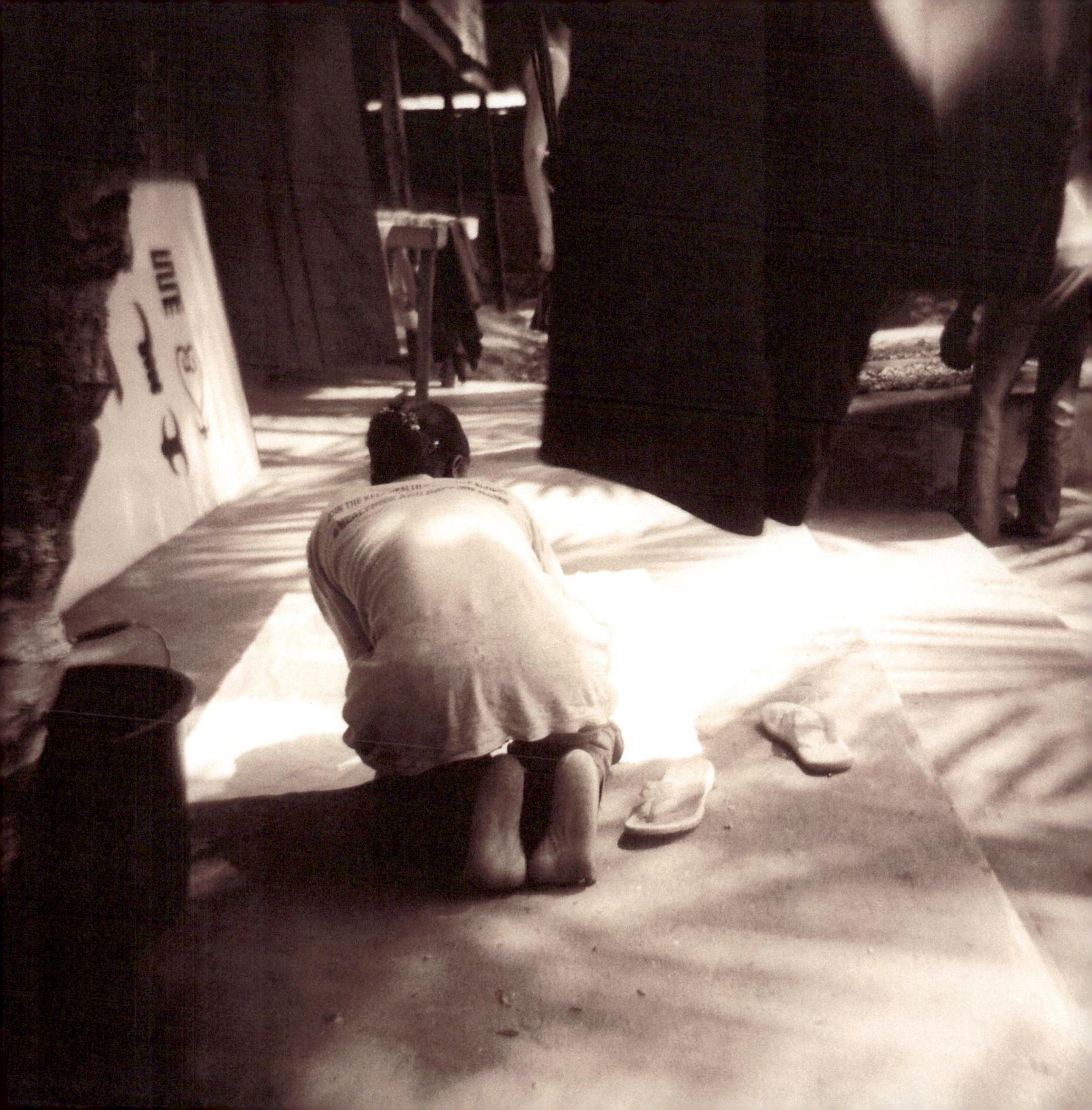

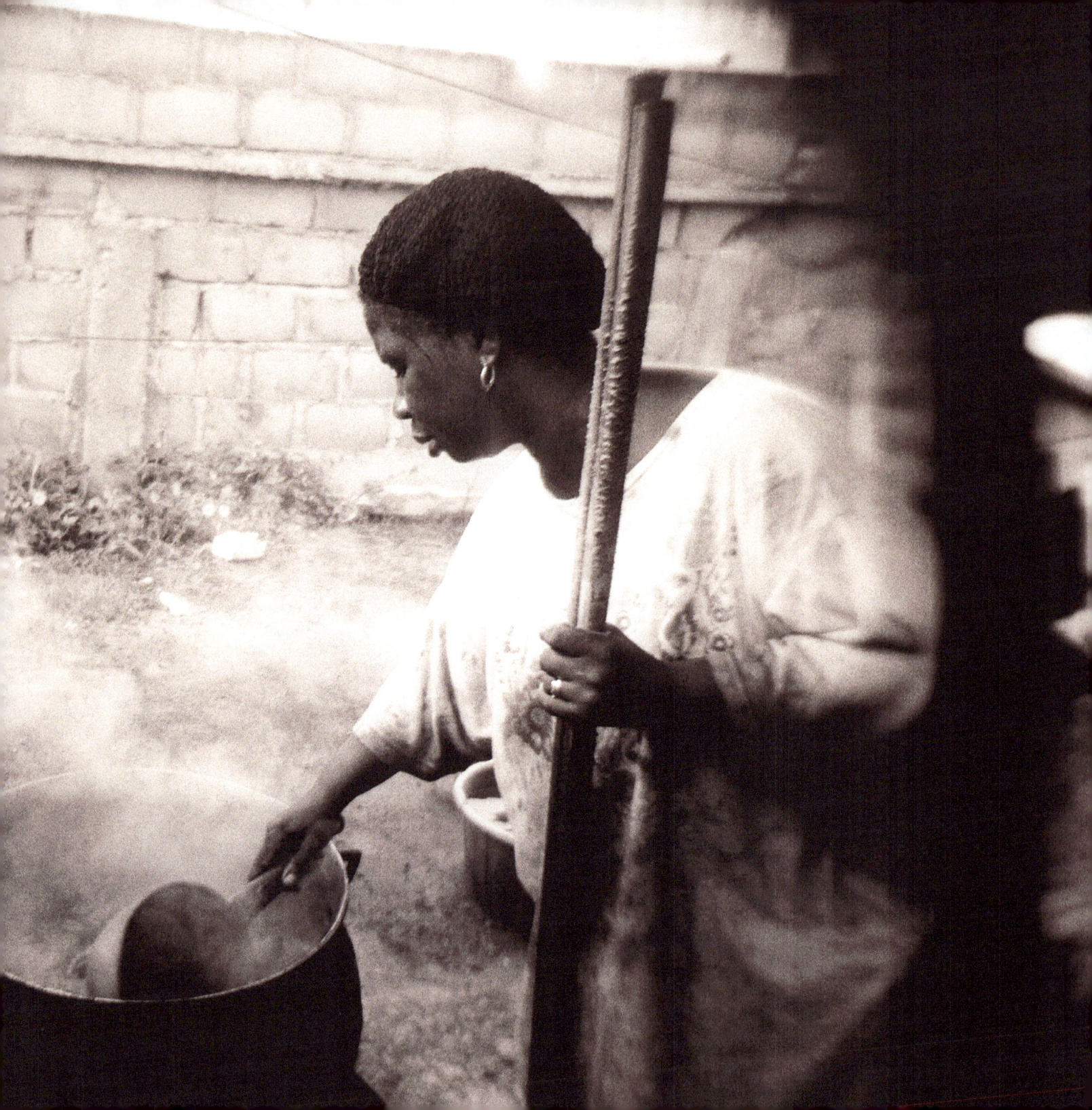

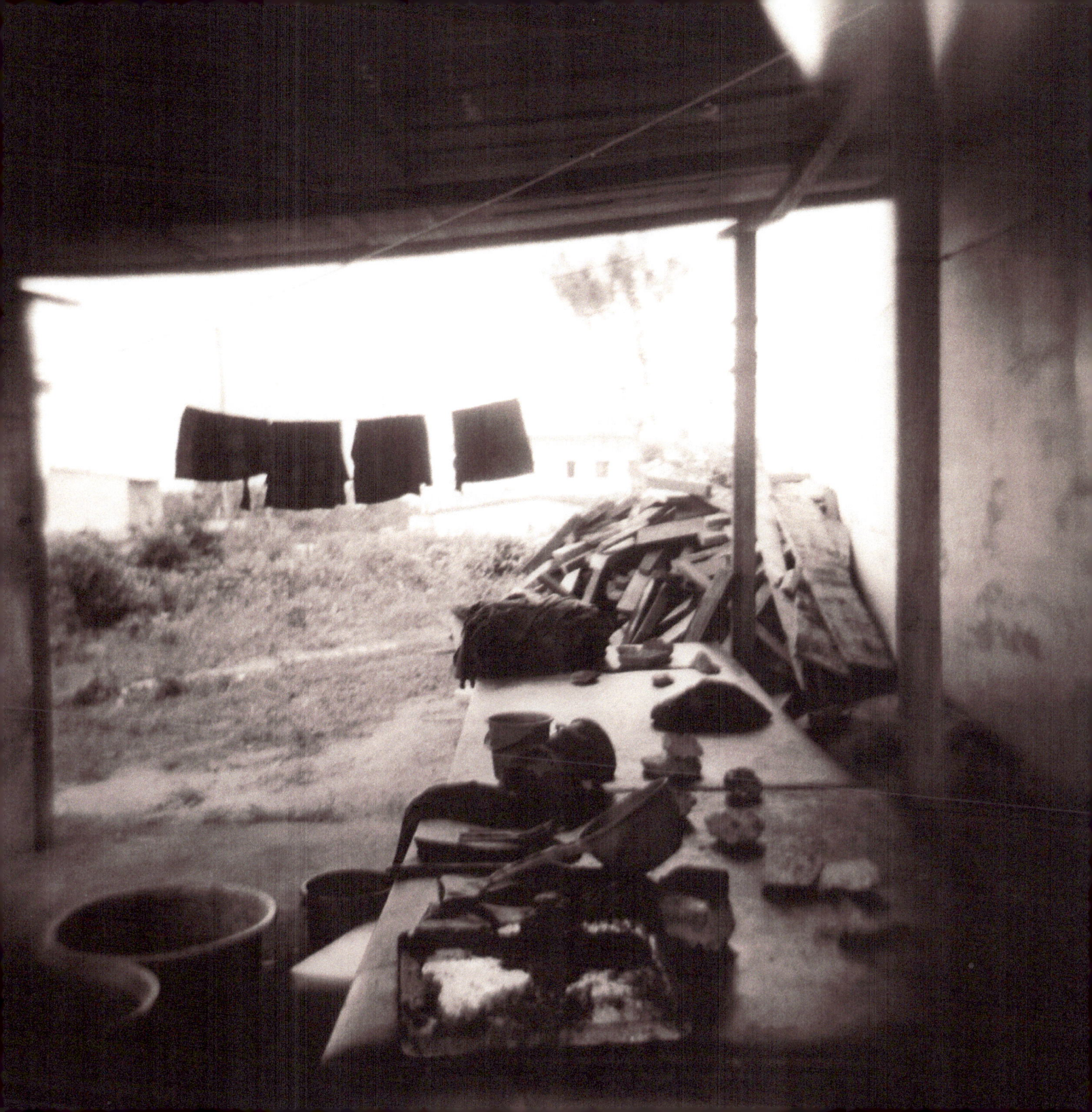

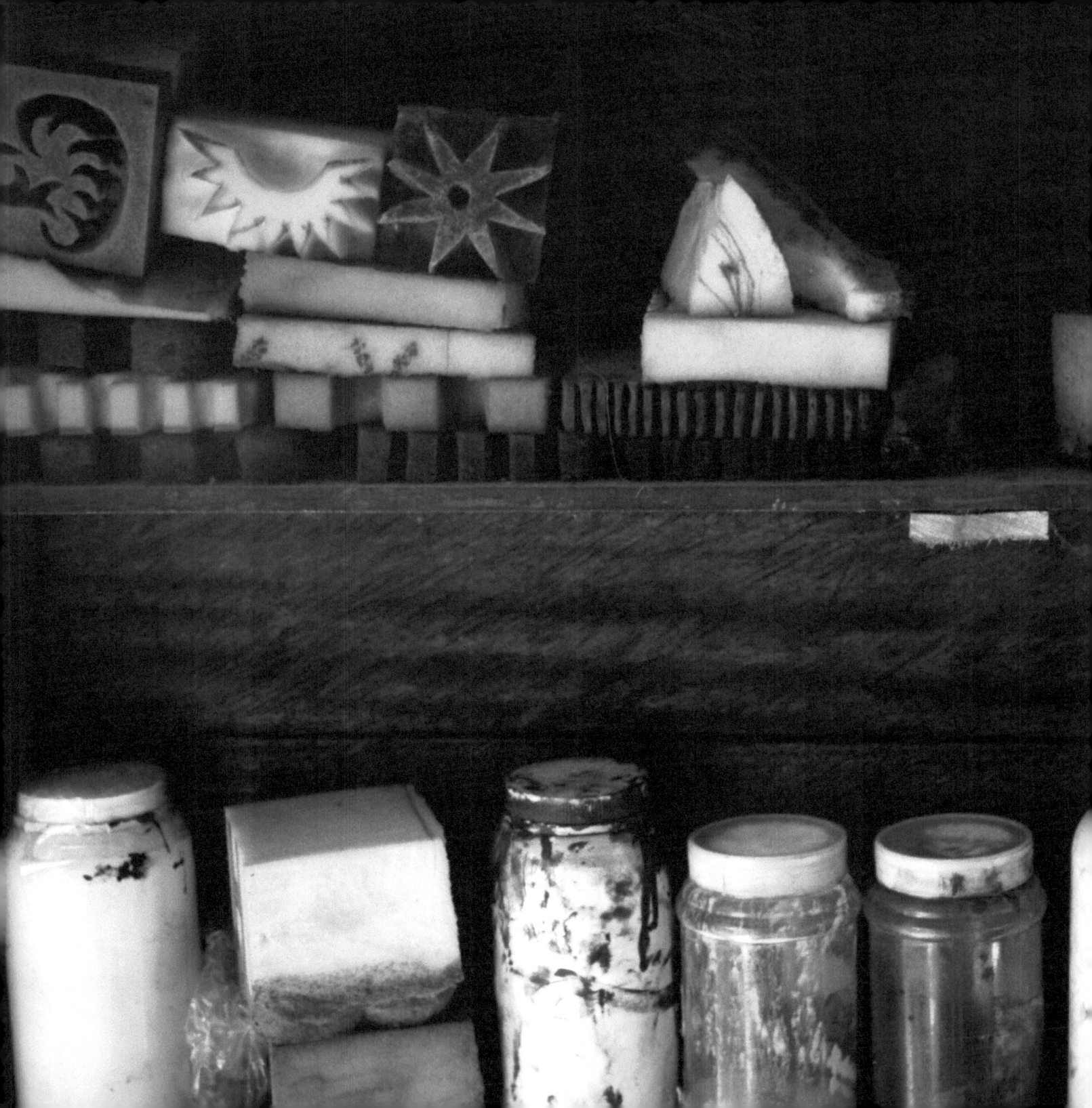

Work Break

After a long day of sorting through bags of batik scraps in the humid office, Mandy, Courtney, Renae and I walk down the street to Casanova, a colorful bar hidden behind a vendor selling egg sandwiches.

A young girl brings out three Star lagers and places a coaster on the glasses. In Ghana coasters go on top to keep the flies out.

Booming voices flood over from the next table. A circle of men holler throughout the evening, pointing dramatically at one another. Renae smiles. "They are regulars. They've been having the same argument for years and they will continue to have the same for the next twenty."

47

Five hours before sunrise…
a faceless man hovers over.

The Muslim chant echoes…
…lost bird, flapping aimlessly
in the wind…

…a larium dream jolts me up.

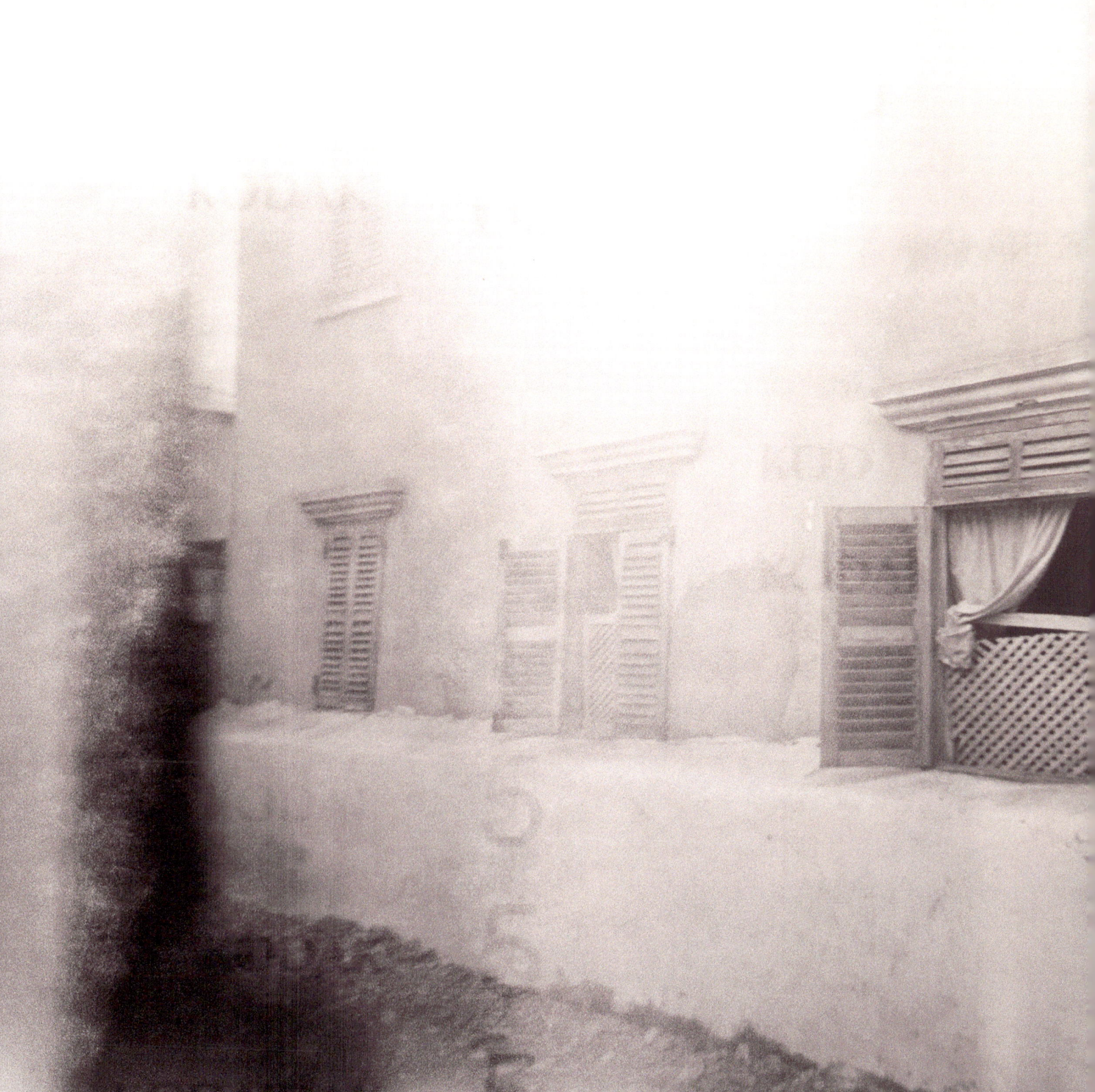

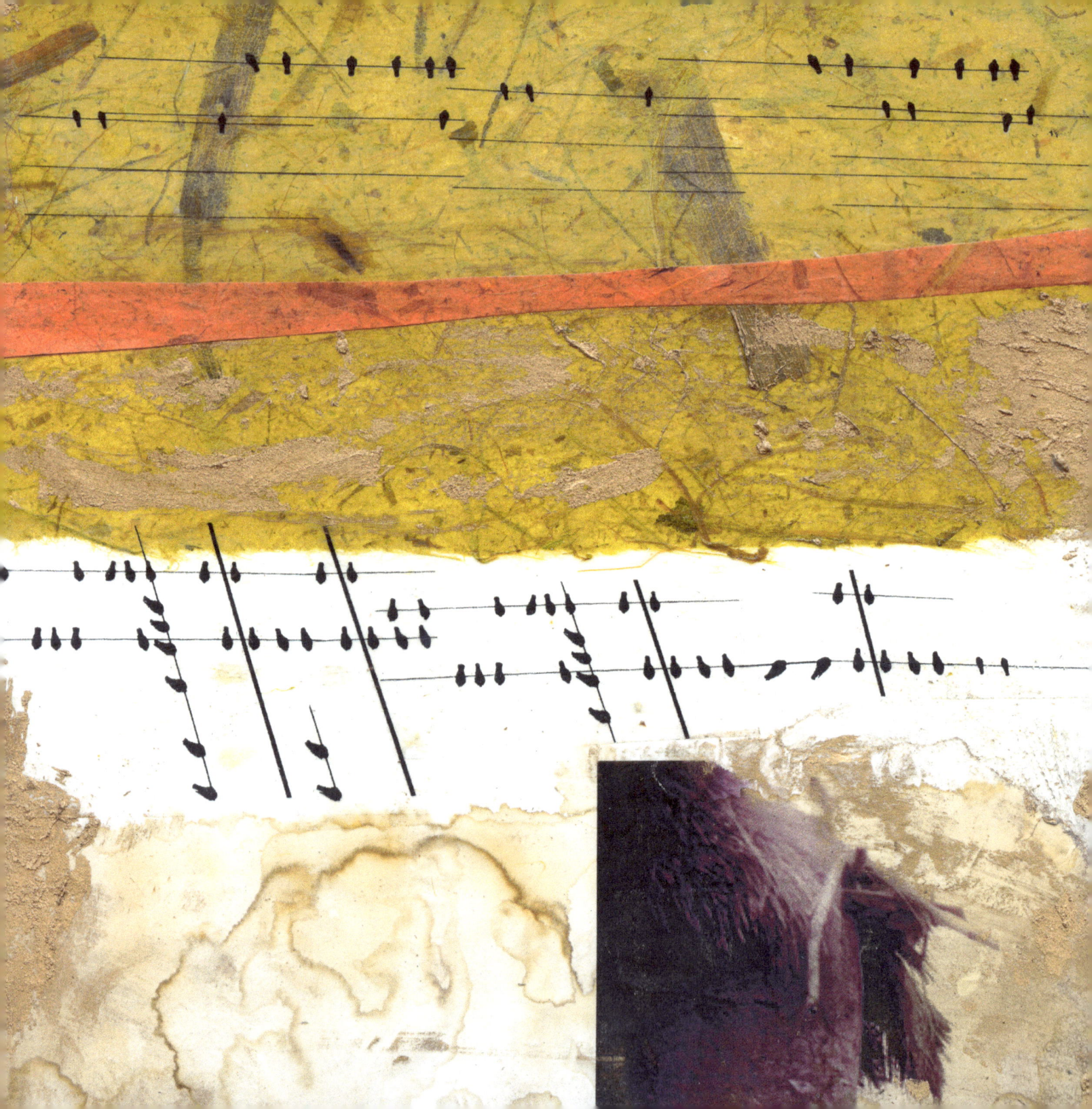

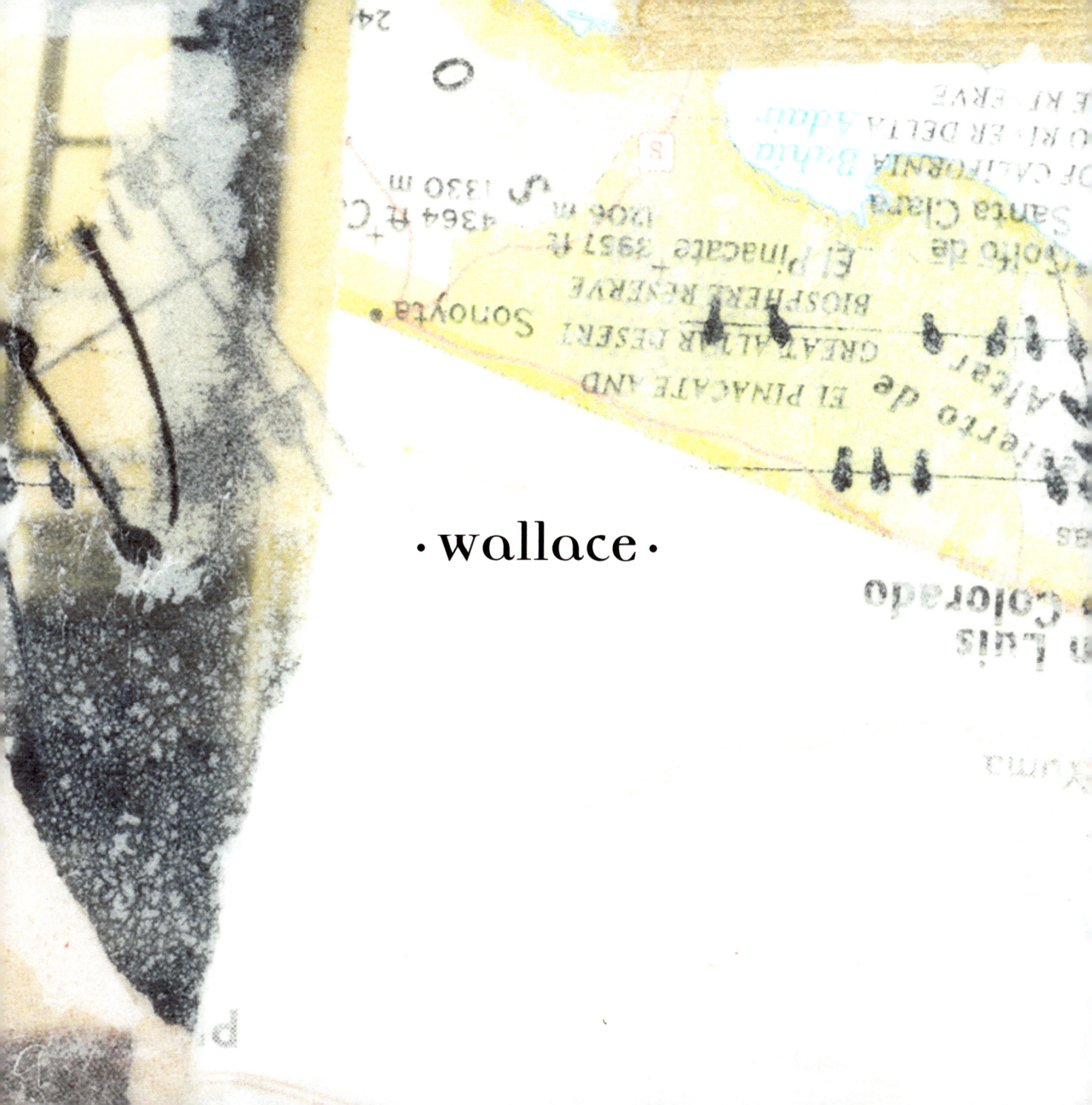

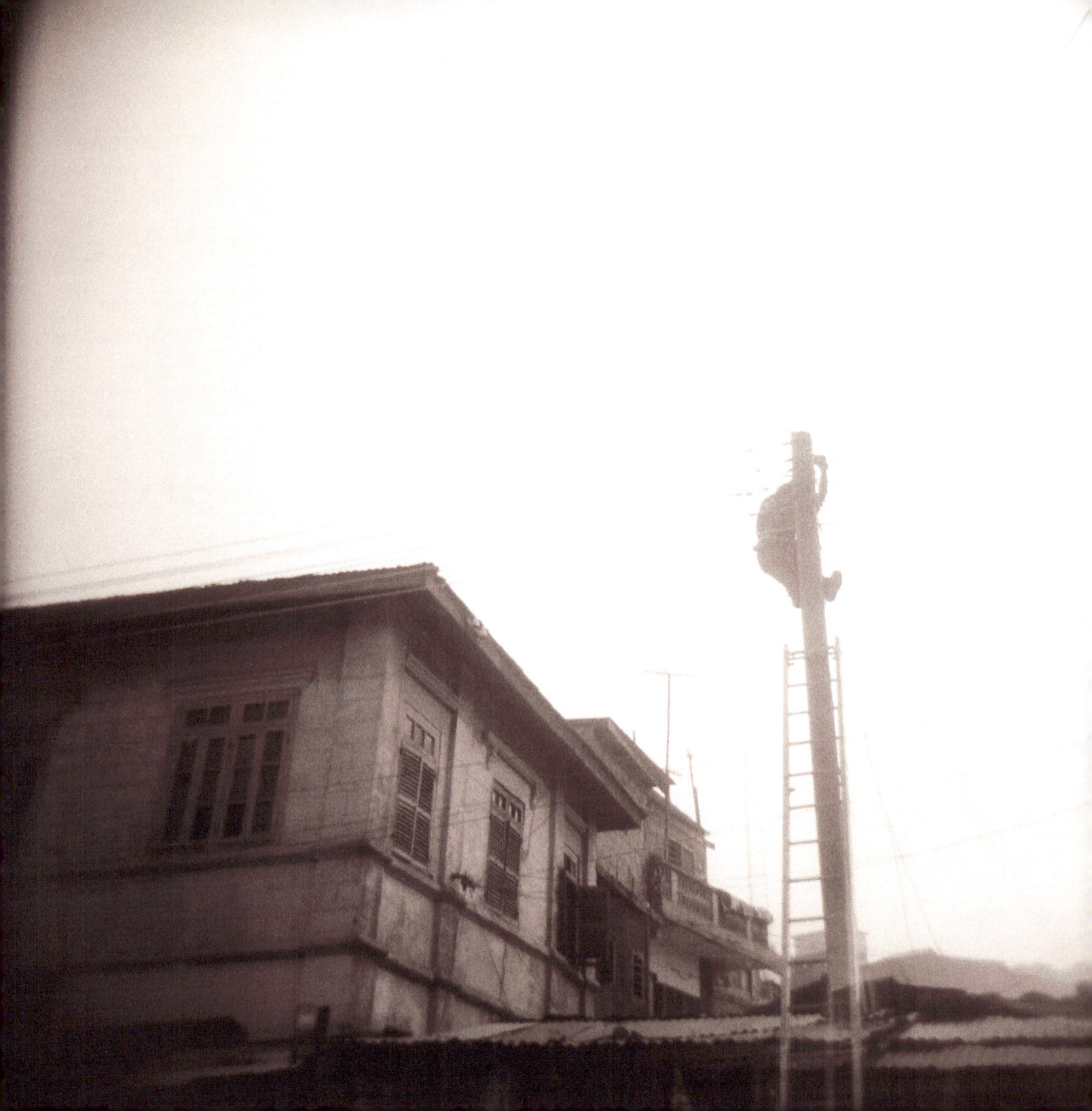

One Man's Perspective

WE KNOW MORE ABOUT YOU THAN YOU KNOW ABOUT US. I WOULD SAY ABOUT 5% OF THE PEOPLE IN THE STATES ARE REALLY INTERESTED IN GHANA.

Wallace's home sits in the nice part of town. With no formal education beyond secondary school, Wallace used a strong business and marketing sense to work his way up from tour guide to governor of the Elmina Slave Castle. He manages the operations in the preserved castle that once held hundreds of slaves destined for the journey to become commodity. He accumulated a small fortune and moved up in the business by selling books about the castle. Kathleen, a volunteer from Georgia, opted to live with the family during her month-long stay in Ghana. Abba, Wallace's wife, is a short, heavy woman. She runs the house. Before Wallace leaves for work, Abba makes him a breakfast of bread, butter, and coffee with condensed milk. A dinner of fufu and soup is on the table when he returns. Although their home is modern in many ways, Wallace follows the tradition of eating alone at the dinner table, while Abba and their three children eat at informal times in the kitchen.

Wallace wanders in after work. He wears a turquoise batiked linen shirt and chews a wood stick. After dinner he reclines with Kathleen, myself, and his family around a James Bond flick.

"Women do most of the work," Wallace divulges as we turn our attention away from the film, "Africa rides on the back of the women." This fact has become common knowledge.

"Have you worked in tourism your whole life?" I ask.

"Oh no," he responds. "I began as a teacher. Tourism in Ghana only began in the late '80s."

"Have you traveled much in Africa?"

Wallace smiles, "It has not always been so easy for Africans to travel from country to country. It is fine for *you* to cross borders, but not for us with a Ghanaian passport. You see, colonialism made it next to impossible to travel from one country to the next. Just near us in Togo, I cannot speak to them because they speak French. Everyone around us speaks French until you reach Nigeria. Plus, you see, years ago it was easier for a Ghanaian to fly to Paris and get a connecting flight to Togo than to pass directly across the border. A person with a passport of influence, like the U.S., will have no problems, but for Africans, it is next to impossible. Too much hassling!"

Wallace flips the chewing stick out of his mouth and looks up toward the ceiling. He continues, expressing his point of view on the States:

"We know more about you than you know about us. I would say about 5% of the people in the States are really interested in Ghana." His hands follow his words. "You control everything. Like global warming. Everybody sees global warming, but you have the power to do something. You have defenses that we do not….in Africa, foreign companies are buying land to grow bananas and other fruits for export. They have their own standards. It is not like a banana in my backyard. They use pesticides and chemicals. Different versions of fruits are harvested on my land."

The Bond movie ends. Wallace's young son flips on a Mexican soap opera poorly dubbed in English.

53

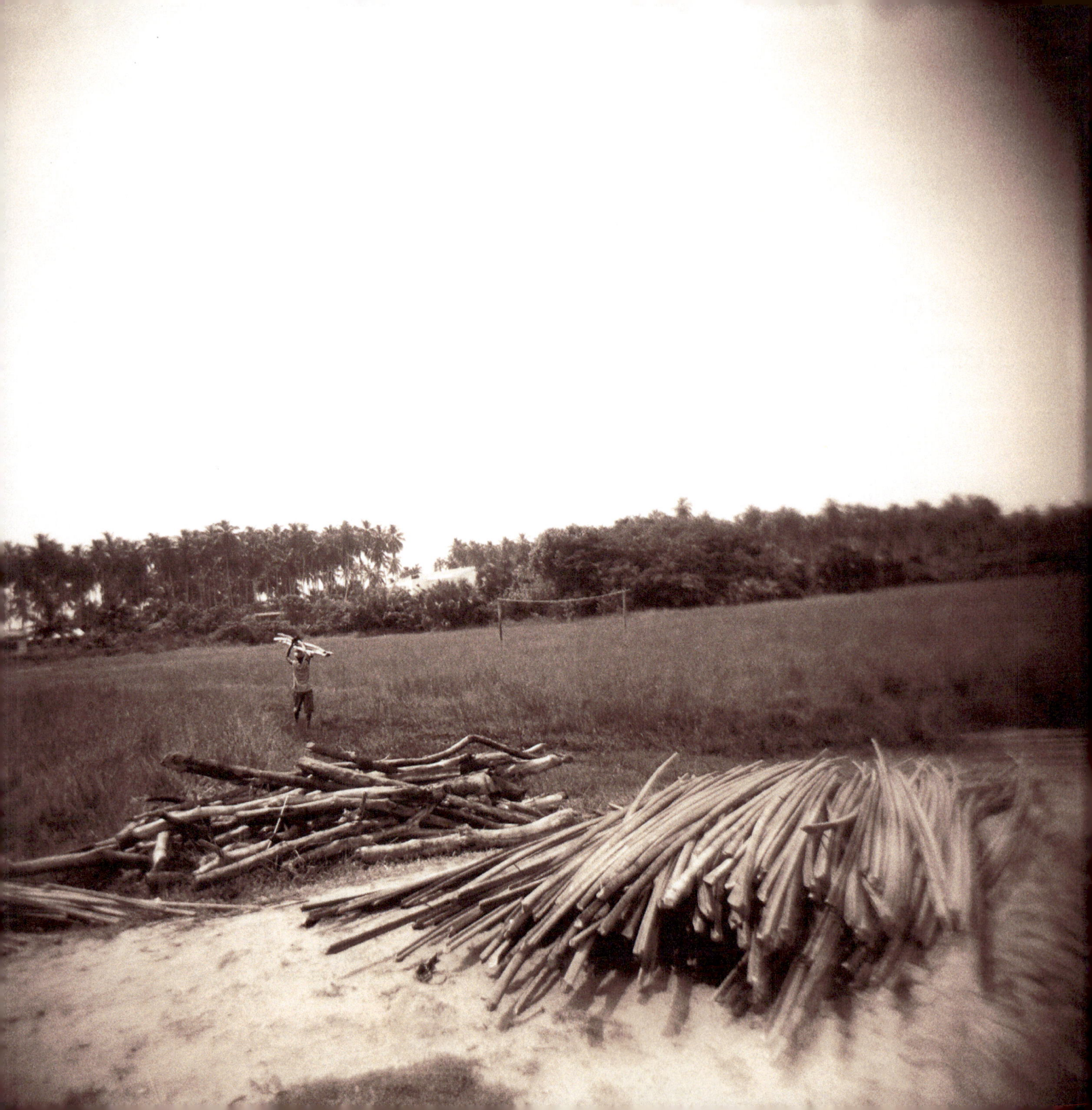

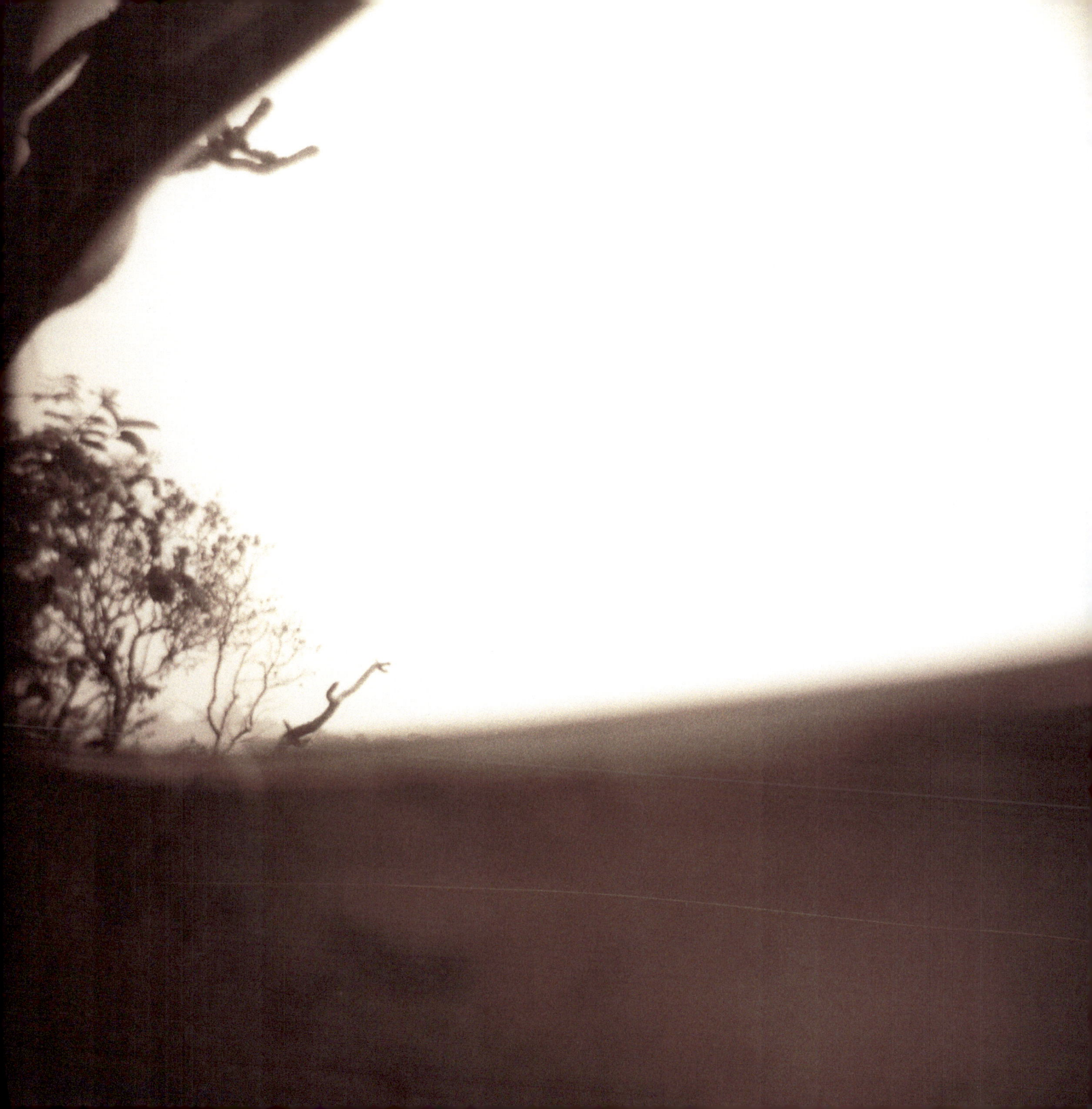

On the street, a man plays a neon green
harmonica while I drink forty cent gin.

Come back, come back,
ccommmme back to mee…

…Ohhhh, come back to me.

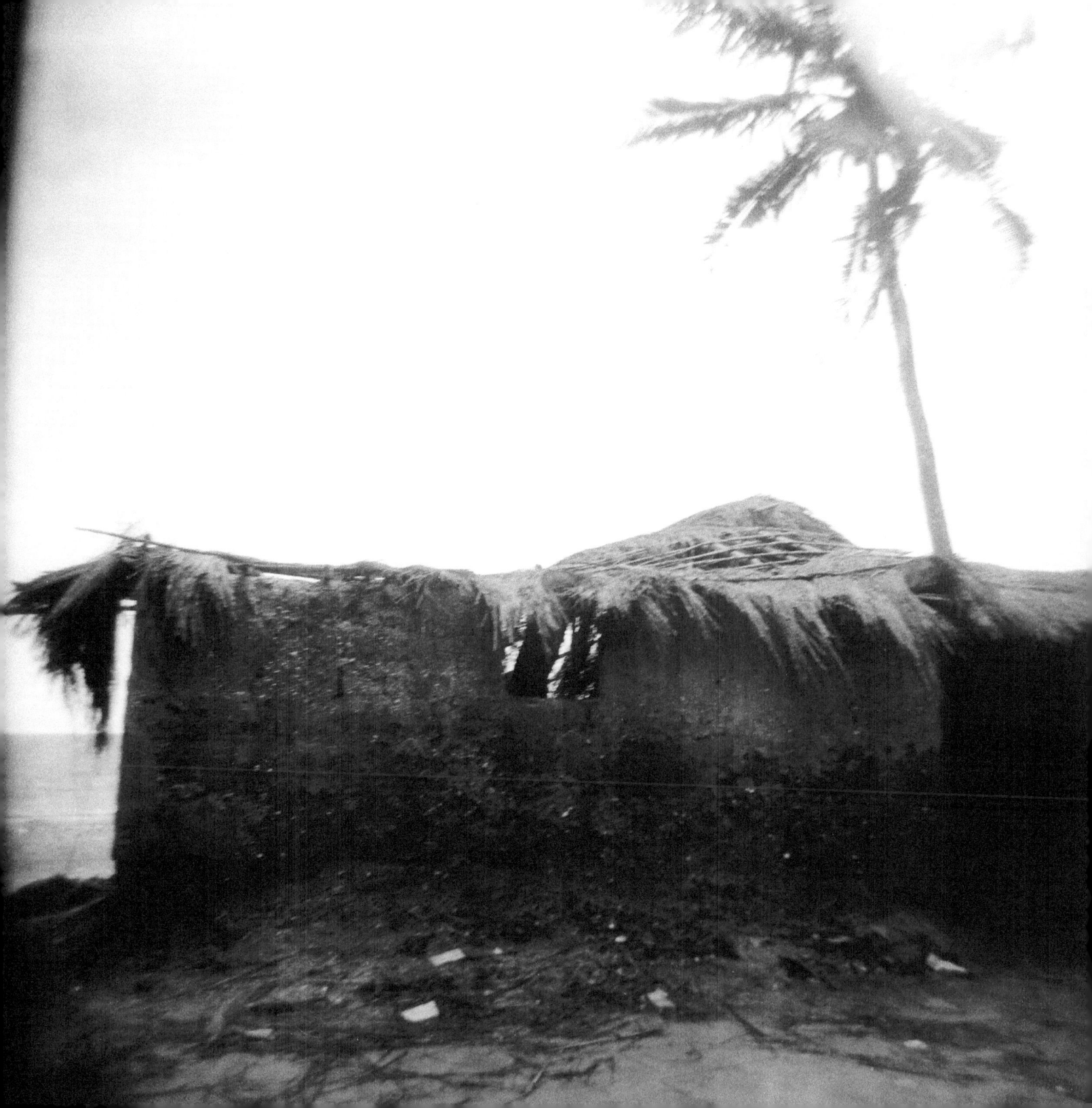

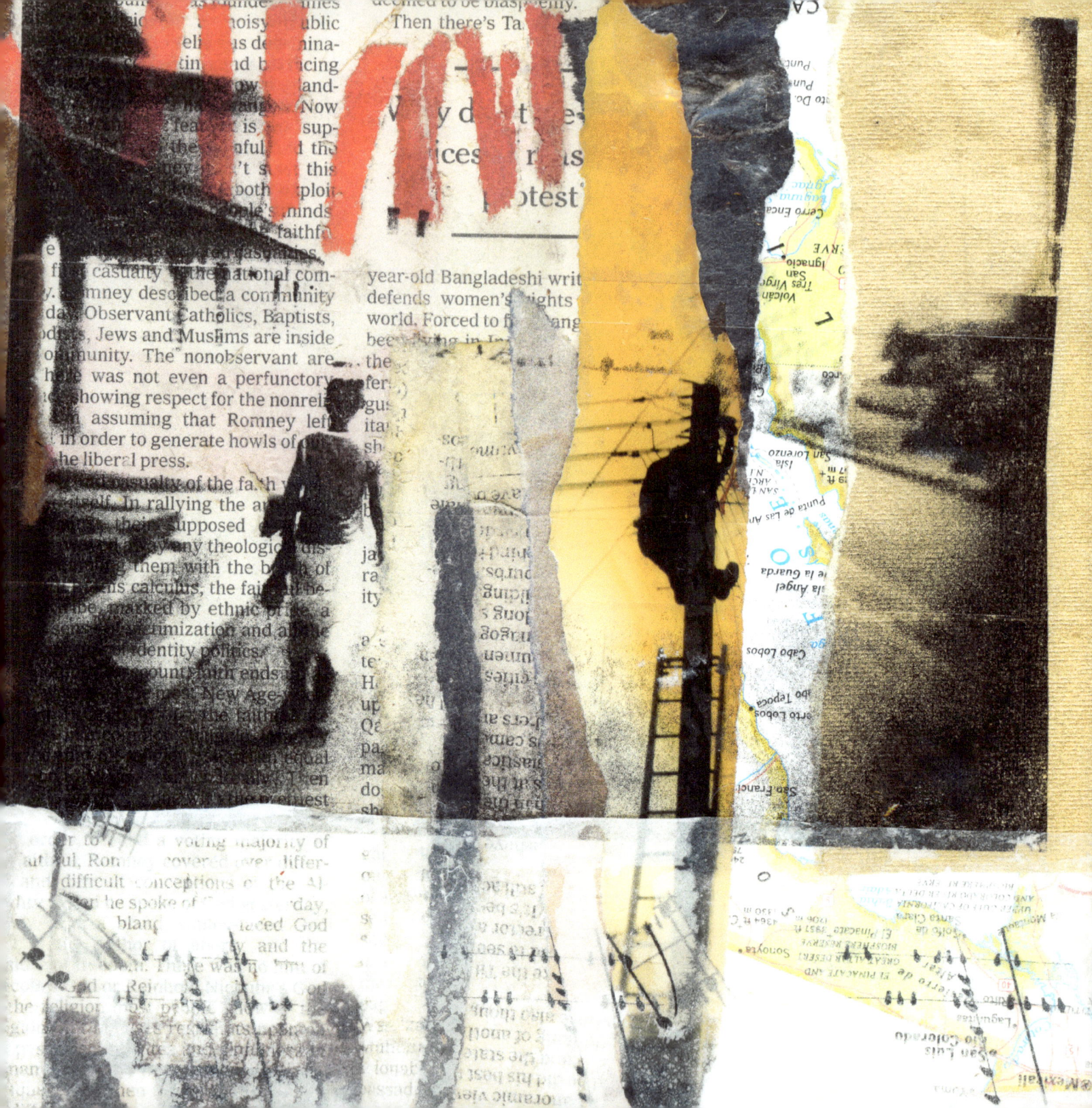

· to and fro ·

The Tro Tro to Cape Coast

My body is tucked tightly against the open window. Wind whips through my body as we speed along the bumpy concrete road. I gradually become totally numb against the air current. Hair darts across my face, now caked in dirt.

My eyes are still tearing from the wind…

"Come, come. Come, come!" A man in tattered white leads me through herds of people selling papaya and fried yam balls.

A boy follows closely beside me. He reaches his hand into my bag. "Hey!" I scream, forcing his hand away.

The leader darts around and hurries me past moving tro tros and human vendors. He squeezes between the white vans, shifting the rearview mirrors aside to sneak me through. I run after him, clutching my purse to my stomach. "Be careful! Watch, watch!" Tro tros ramble through the wave of movement. "Come, come…this way!"

An elderly man counts ticket money at a wooden booth. For 25,000 cedi ($2.50) he issues me a scrap of manila paper, my ticket back to Cape Coast.

The leader smiles. "You will thank me now for my kind service." I nod. I pass him a bill for 5,000. "I am Tony!" We butt fists and he dashes away.

I clutch my bag in front of me and file into a hot vehicle. Scrunched in the back corner, I sit between the window and a young girl and plop my heavy bag on my lap. People crowd the car selling cookies, gum, ice water, and coconut juice in metal bowls hoisted on their heads. The young girl purchases a bag of cold yogurt in a pink package. She breaks a hole in the end with her teeth and sucks out the contents. My body is tucked tightly against the open window. I hang my arm outside to create a pale white flag. Vendors crowd the vehicle

at each stop, chasing after the van with ice water and pineapple. Wind whips through my body as we speed along the bumpy concrete road. My limbs turn to water. I gradually become totally numb against the air current. Hair darts across my face, now caked in dirt. Thumps echo in my ears as the tro tro decelerates at intervals where policemen in black uniforms inspect each passing car.

Bloodshot eyes peer at me beneath fluorescent-colored hard hats. Stores sell household goods with names like IN HIM IS LIFE and JESUS SAYS SO. Vendors carry checkered brown purses on each arm. White men stand in front of factories, barking into mobile phones. Iron gates sit beside love seats, for sale on the side of the road. Black exhaust suffocates the back of the tro tro. A pastor introduces himself. He chronicles his year-long trip to the States in 1993. Three hours later we arrive in Cape Coast.

The steady sound of rain beats in tune with the hum of the air conditioner. Every other minute the rooster crows in the distance. In each corner of the office a brown puddle forms. Ants crawl over computers and tangled knots of wire. Outside, the dirt roads become swamps of wet clay. As Agnes, Teresa, and Matilda arrive at the office, more and more brown footsteps track on the tile floor. Folks walk by holding colorful umbrellas with plaid designs. A woman selling pastries drapes a white towel over her head. Water leaks into her plexi-enclosed case of baked goods.
The slow morning pace begins.

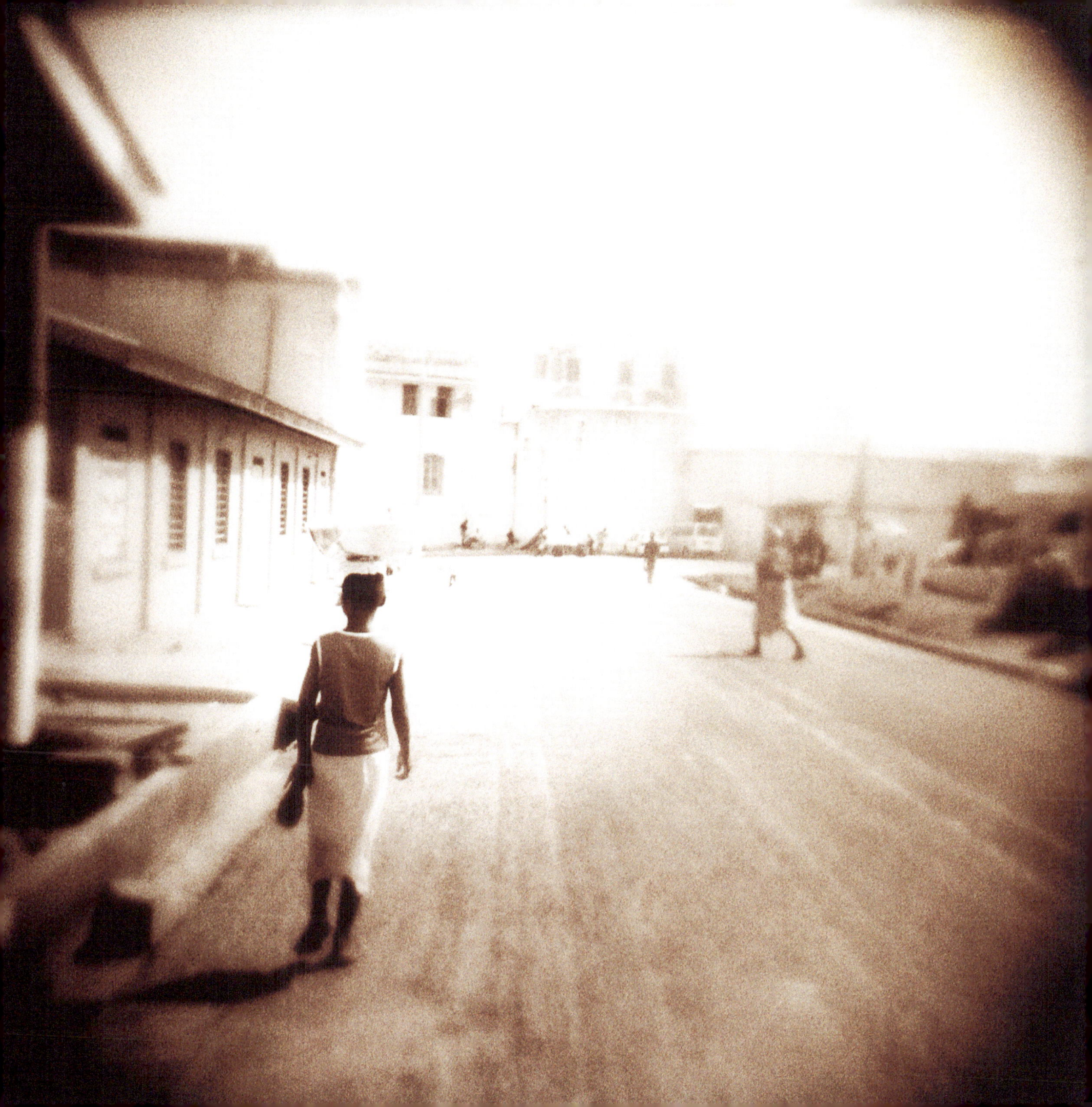

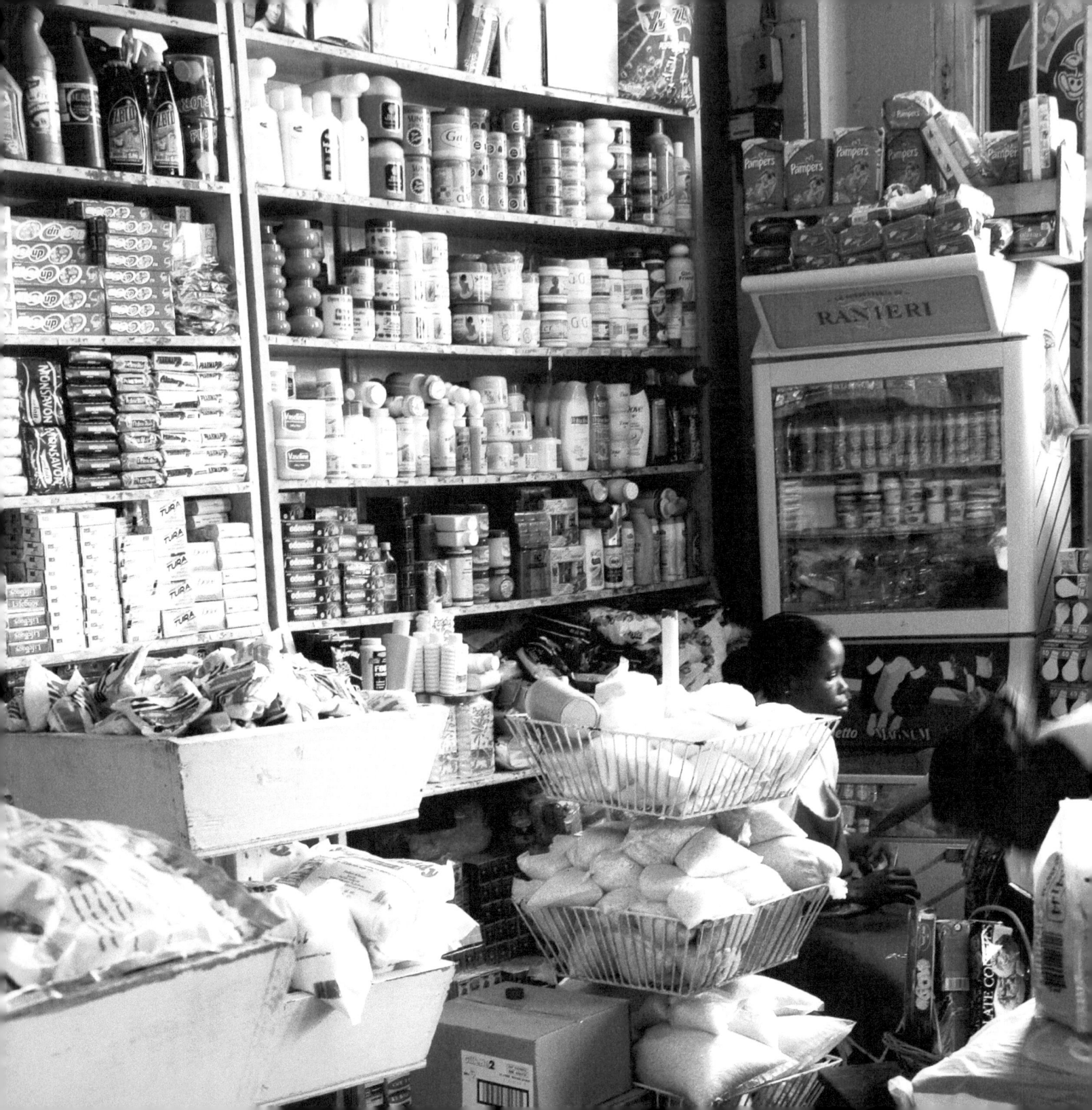

DRIVING PAST THE
FISHING VILLAGE IN
THE EARLY MORNING,
THE SMELL OF SEAWATER
COMBINES WITH MUSTY
UPHOLSTERY TO CREATE
THE ILLUSION OF SMOKY
MUSTARD. PIECES OF
BROWN FOAM DANGLE
DOWN FROM THE CEILING
OF THE TRO TRO.

Market Wisdom

Sunday morning marks the giant "Brunie Wewu" market day. The title translates to "white man trash". Vendors spread throws in front of wood kiosks. Old shoes, blue jeans, pirated DVDs, tools, and suitcases line the street.

I bundle my bags in front of me and scrunch between two thin men. Their seats are balanced unsteadily on a narrow metal rod. I sit on the rod and plant my feet into the metal floor.

The tro tro stops at the central market, the nucleus of the city's chaos. Men sell newspapers on a wide, wheel drawn cart for 4000 cedi. Others shovel mud and trash out of the sewers. A thin boy walks slowly past me. He wears a siren red shirt that reads I PICK MY NOSE in bold, black letters.

Passport Renewal

"ARE YOU THE PAPARAZZI?"
THE MAN GRUMBLES,
INDICATING MY CAMERA
WITH HIS EYES.

After sixty days I dutifully report to a thickly built Ghanaian official in a dark green suit. A can of powdered milk sits in the corner of a dim salmon office. A woman sits at an adjacent desk in an identical uniform. She focuses her concentration on a stack of papers as I walk in. A triangle of light glows around the officer's desk.

He looks through my stash of papers: an application, a letter from Women in Progress, passport photos, flight itinerary, passport, and 100,000 cedis.

"B-L-A-U-K-O-P-F," he articulates in a long, slow breath. "What does it mean?"

"Bluehead."

"Heh, heh… Bluehead? In what language?"

"Austrian German I suppose."

"Are you Austrian?"

"No, but someone in my family was."

"I see."

He slides the documents into a folder, including the passport. "You come back Thursday for this."

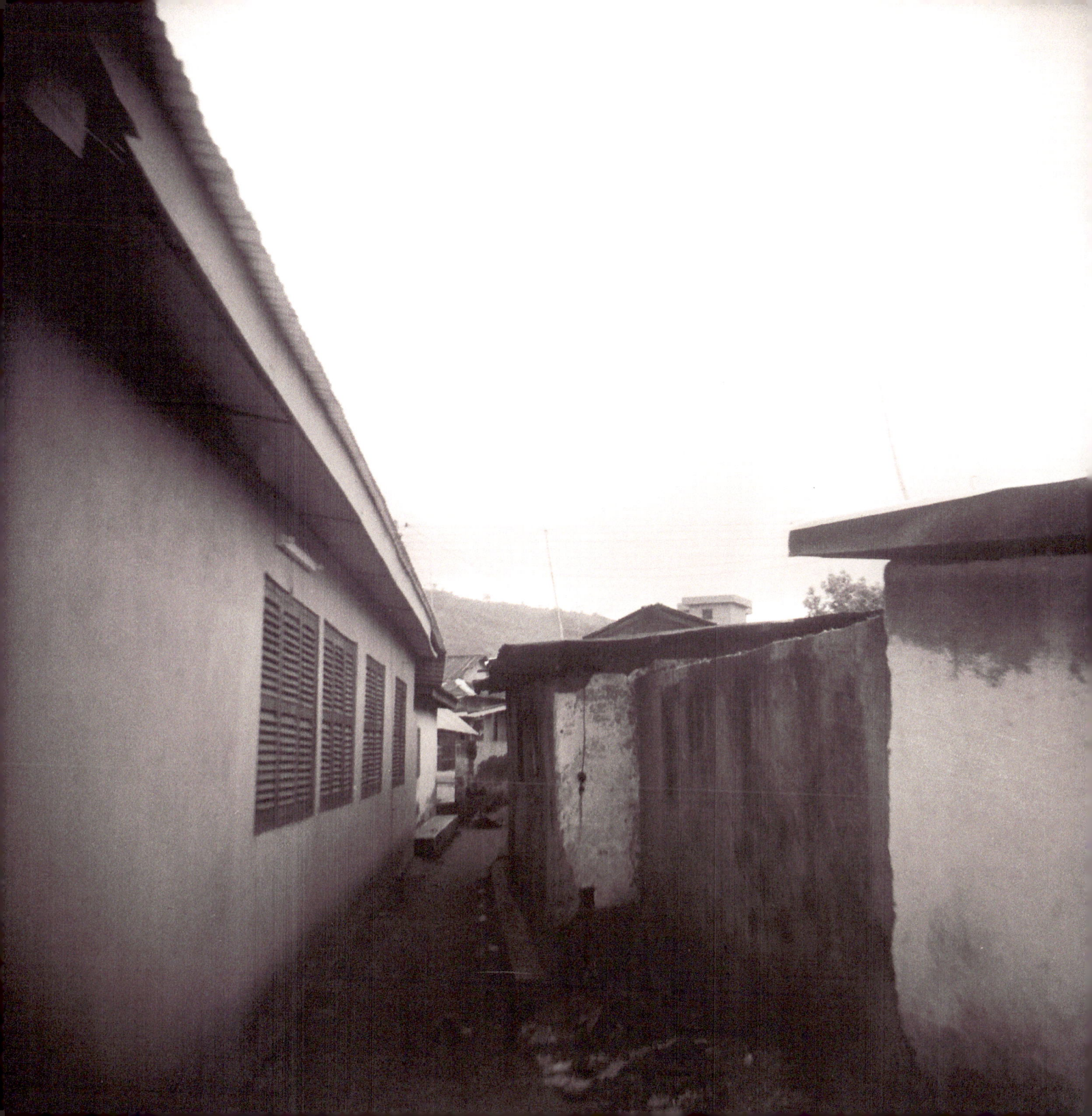

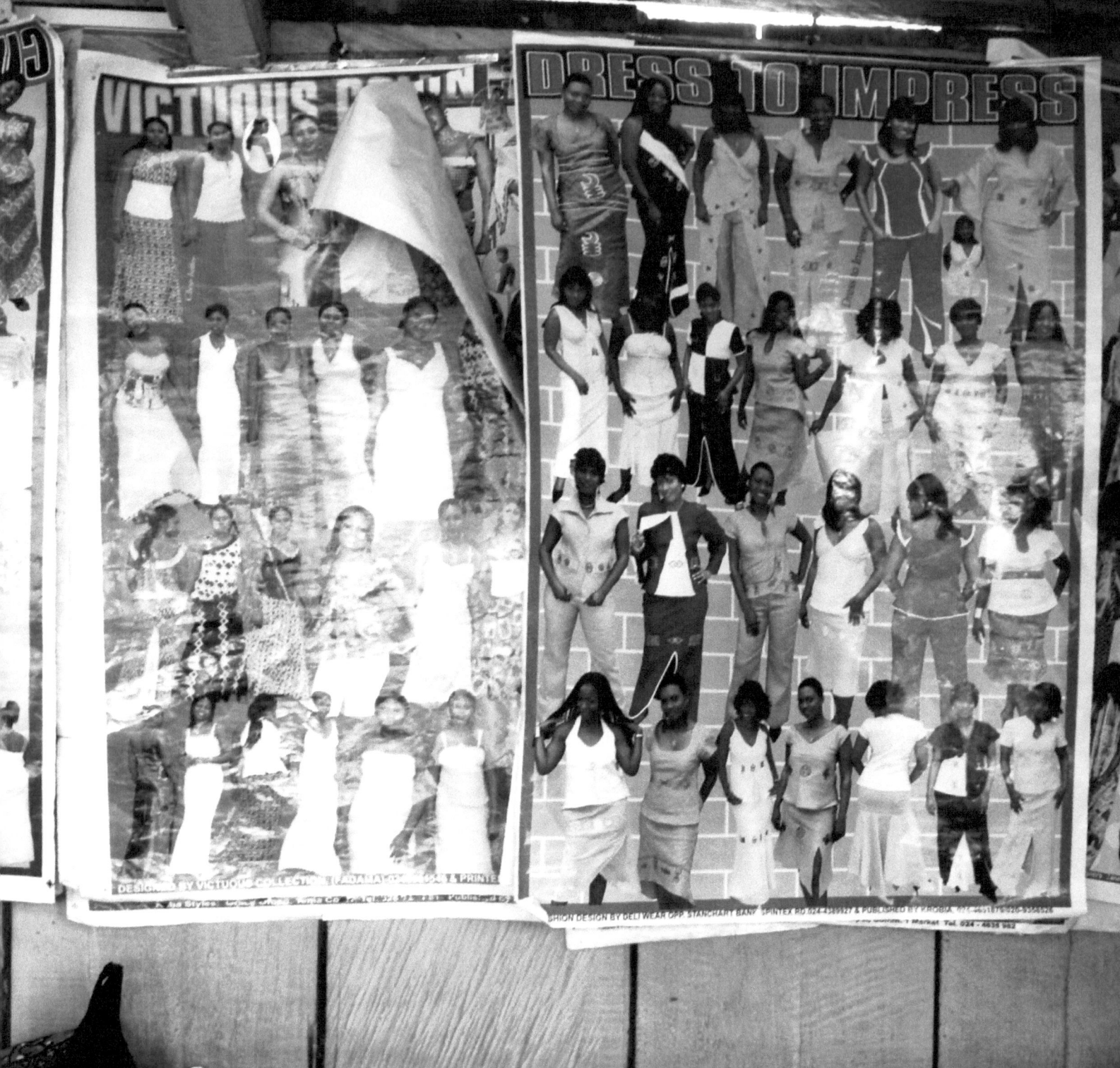

Male Organ Missionary

A MIDDLE-AGED HOW-TO-GUIDE SALESMAN IN BLUE STEPS ONTO THE FRONT OF A CROWDED BREED OF TRO TRO BUS. FOR 5000 CEDI, HE SELLS WISDOM.

"Please, if your male organ is not working well, go and buy honey and an onion. Boil the onion until it is soft and add the honey. The quantity is here!" A middle-aged how-to-guide salesman in blue steps onto the front of a crowded tro tro bus. The man waves green and pink pamphlets in the air like a Christian missionary preaching the Bible. He reads snippets aloud in an enticing advertisement for name meanings, zodiac symbols, and male reproductive remedies.

The pink pamphlet depicts a happy couple embracing. A mint green pamphlet reveals the true meaning of names. For 5,000 cedi, he sells wisdom. Your Book of Life Map informs me that "Julia" means dazzling and lovely.

…bumpidump…bummmmmmm…

The odor of poop and body odor filters past damp bodies. Men point their fingers toward the driver seat like guns. I sit, scrunched in the tro tro, as if in an ant farm. Hanging from the rearview mirror, the Virgin Mary gazes at the crowd. Gospel music blares on the speakers.

The tro tro rambles out of the market leaving behind the chaos of vendors, vans, and brown shell eggs.

…oh Lord, save thee our grace… bummmm… burmmmmm…

A frail man beside me wears a navy baseball cap decorated in gold stitching.

"How long is the trip to Amedzofe Falls?" I holler over the noise of the engine.

"Yes!" he nods.

"No, how long? One hour, two, ten?"

"Yeah!!"

A choir belts out to the honking car horns. We follow a purple taxi called IT COULD BE YOU out of the city toward Amedzofe Falls.

As the congestion clears, the driver flips the cassette tape over. A woman with a beautiful scratchy voice sings pop-y island music.

Below a brown air vent, a bumper sticker declares ALL POWER BELONGS TO JESUS. The vehicle was meant for the junkyard ten years ago. It trudges up a hill, packed with ten bodies too many. Inside, the car is a sea of patterns in golds, blues, and reds. We are like a string of beads tangled together in a messy ball of thread.

goat for sale…

We bump over red tinted roads surrounded by green stalks toward a lush mountain.

A man in a yellow, red, and black cubist print shirt reads about the Year of the Pig. "He is sensitive and makes life-long friends."

The boy beside me explains that the Parliament Chief died and the mountain village was mourning the death. Groups of people in decadent red robes celebrate along the side of the road; their faces are painted in red and black.

"When did the chief die?"

"Two years ago," he replies matter-of-factly.

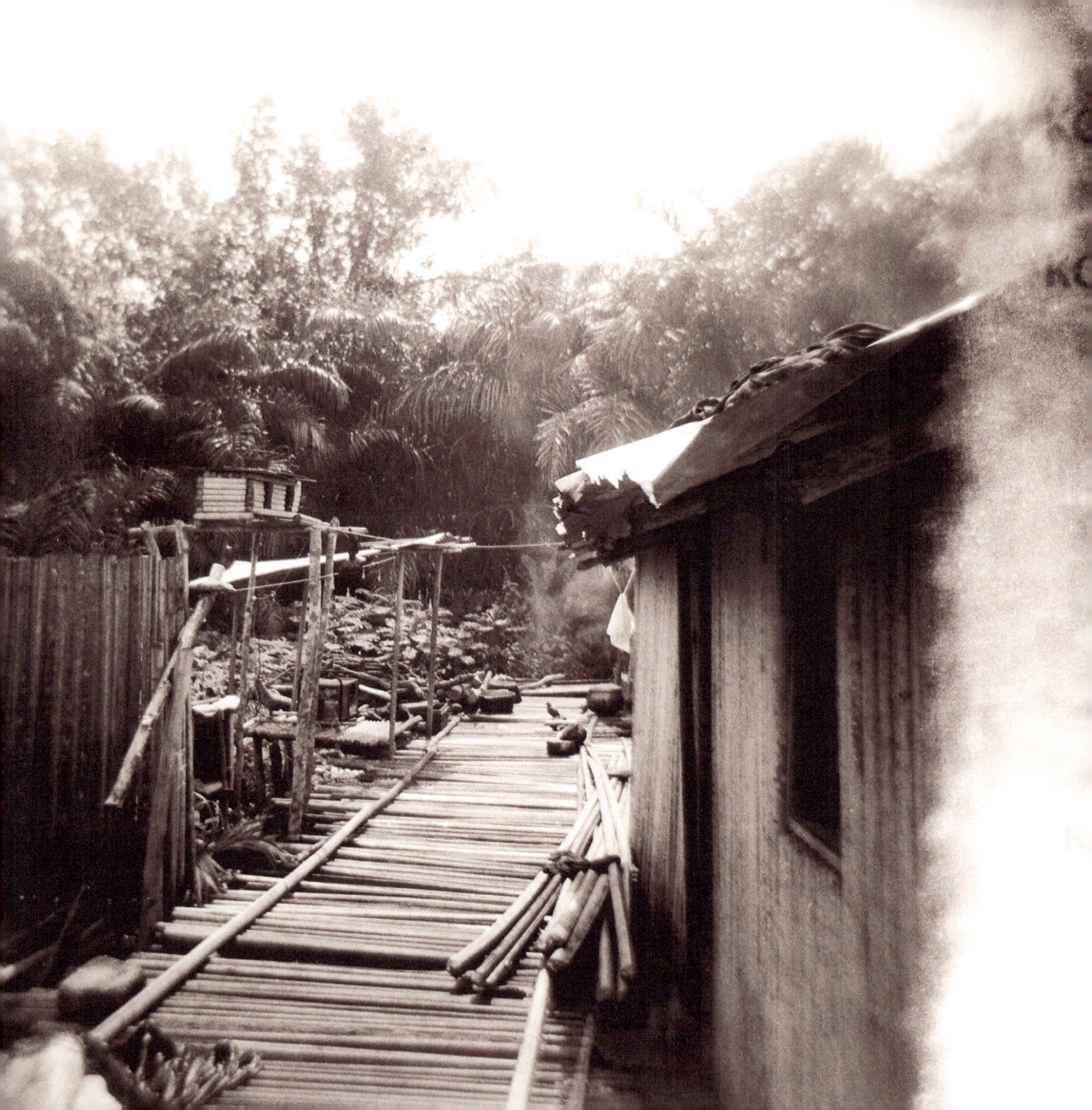

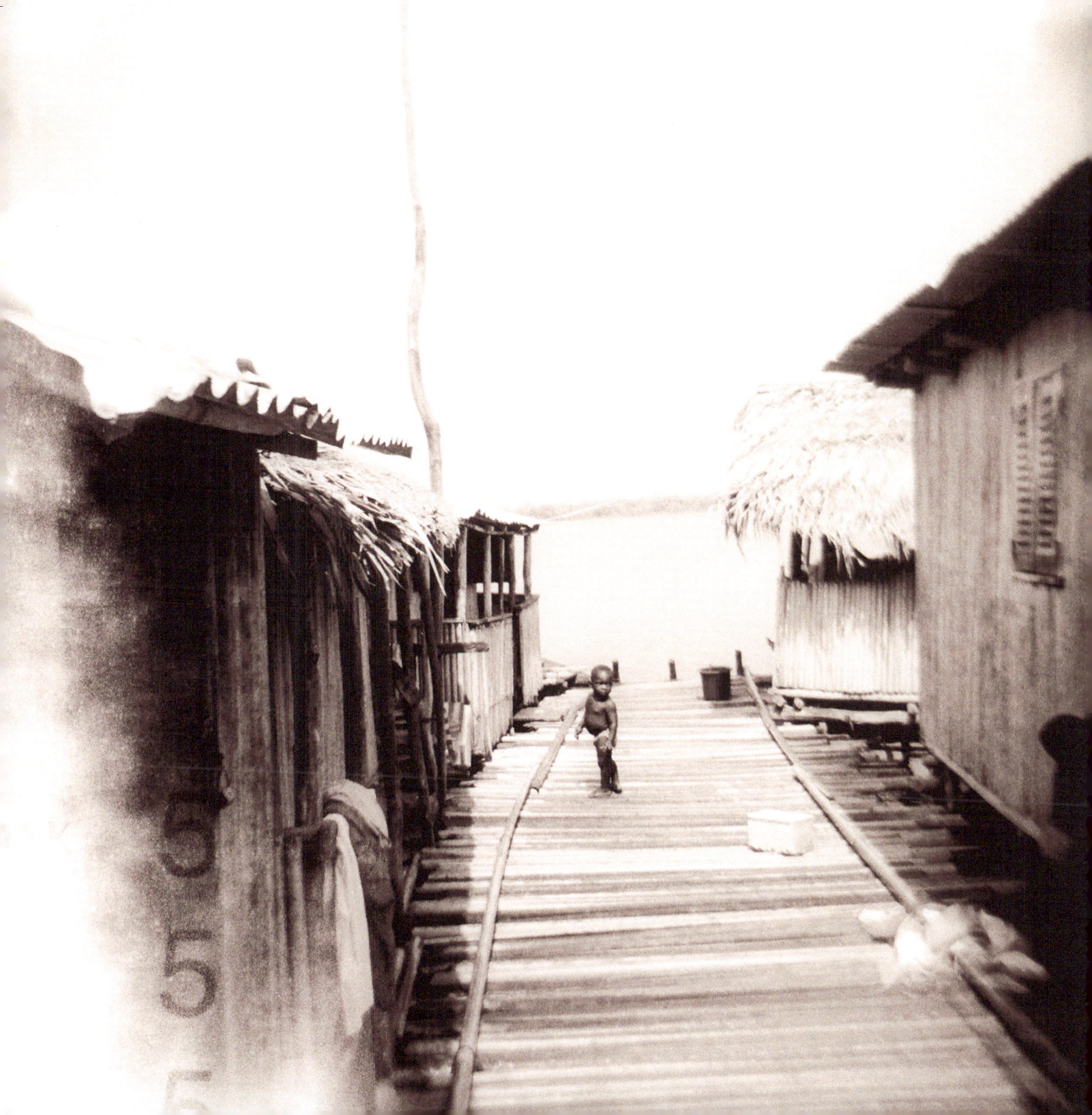

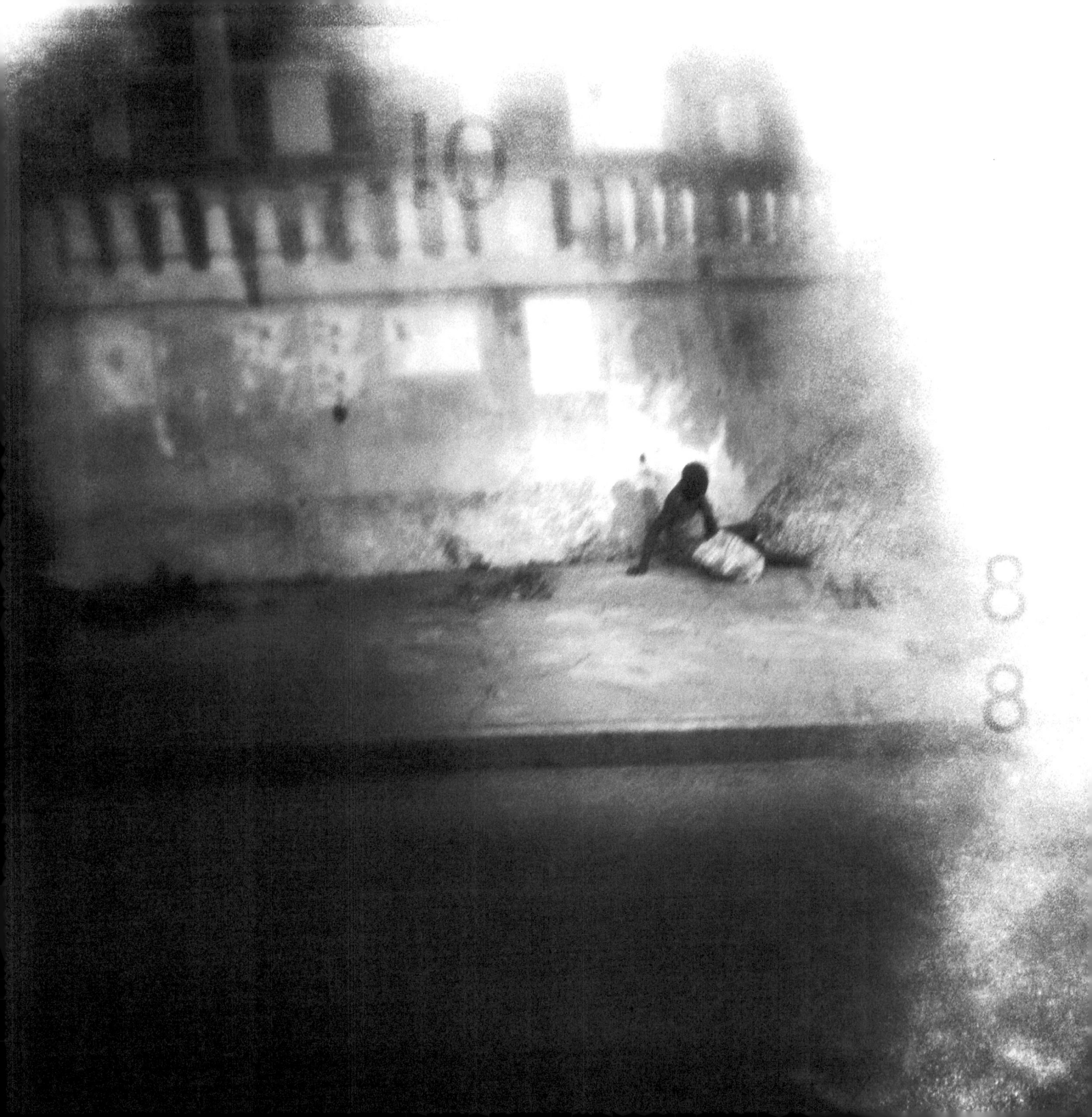

Snapshot

MY BODY IS TREMBLING.
I REACT MINDLESSLY.
I NEED TO GET AWAY
FROM THE SCENE. IT
DIDN'T FEEL LIKE I
WAS CRYING, BUT MY
EYES ARE WET.

She rages toward me without warning. I had just raised my camera to snap a photo of a sign covered in smoke.

"Do not take my picture!" A woman wearing a long red dress runs toward me shrieking. She wraps her arms around me in a tight, angry hold.

"Do not take my picture!" she screams incessantly in a thick, shrill tone.

I cling to my bag. She tries to snatch the small camera out of my grip.

"No!" I think I shout. "I did not take your picture!" It is true. I don't see her until she flies toward me. She lunges for the camera, gripping my arms tightly. I refuse to let go.

Suddenly she swings back. A man pulls her to the ground. My body is trembling. I react mindlessly. I need to get away from the scene. The woman breaks away from the Ghanaian man. A crowd runs over. I dart into the main road. The first lane is empty. I run across a grass patch island to the opposing side and fling my arm in the air to call a taxi. No one drives past. A small group of men run toward me from across the street.

"You ok? You ok?"

"I didn't take her picture!" I cry, "She thought I took her picture, but I didn't!" A security guard in a brown uniform pulls me across toward a pink hotel. "Do you have everything? Make sure you have all your items!"

More men surround me. "You ok? You ok?"

It didn't feel like I was crying, but my eyes are wet. The guard runs toward the woman who is blocked from my view by a mass of men. They grab my arm and pull me in different directions. Their voices blend together. "Come this way, come this way… just let her leave… where do you want to go?"

"Are you sure you have everything?" The guard has reappeared. "Check everything!"

My purse is bulging with cedi bills. I feel my camera, film, and small journal. "Yes, I have everything. Please, I just want to go." I have calmed down, but the surrounding commotion continues. Drops of sweat cloud my eyes.

"Where do you want to go?" a man in purple says gently.

"East Cantoments." I say the first place that came to mind. The guard starts to pull me over, but then yields to the crowd.

"Follow me. Come." A thin driver wearing a clean white oxford shirt leads me to his taxi.

"Did you lose this?" A bald man shoves a book through the window. "Is this yours?" He holds a Bible with a pamphlet of Mary on the side.

"Nope."

The driver pulls out in the busy intersection. "Oh! Sorry, sorry!" He looks back at me with genuine concern. "That woman, that woman was not Ghanaian! She was a refugee from Liberia!" His eyes look as sad as mine. "Please, forget!" We drive toward a busy circle. "Forget, forget."

I sit motionless until we reach East Cantoments. The driver plays the radio. He taps his hands on the steering wheel to lighten the mood. As I hop out of the car he looks back. "Please, please," he utters, "Nobody will ever hurt you again. No more."

71

On the back of a spotless white car, AMERICA HAS MORALS is scrawled on a bumper sticker.

Leopard print upholstery covers the inside seats and steering wheel.

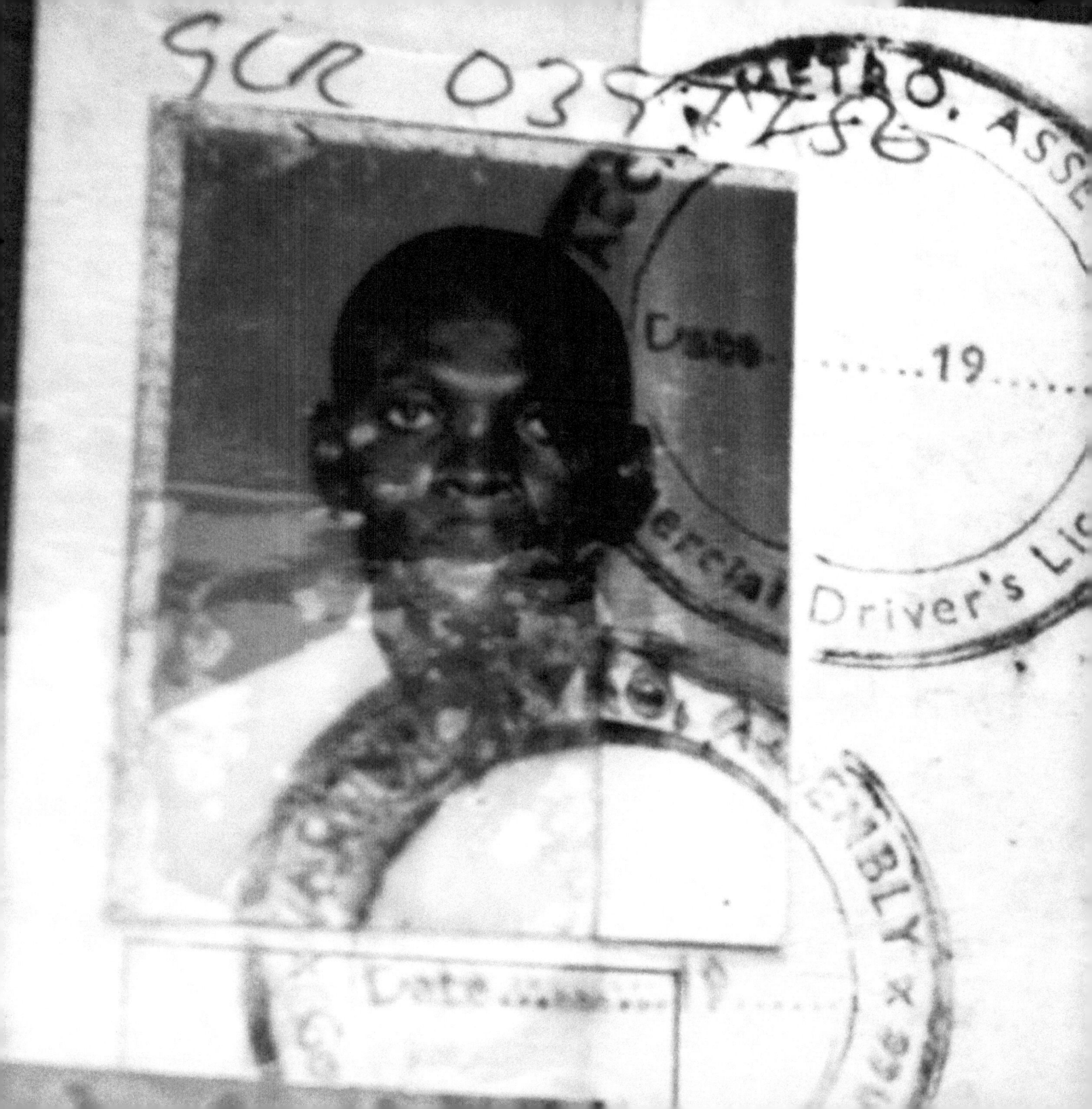

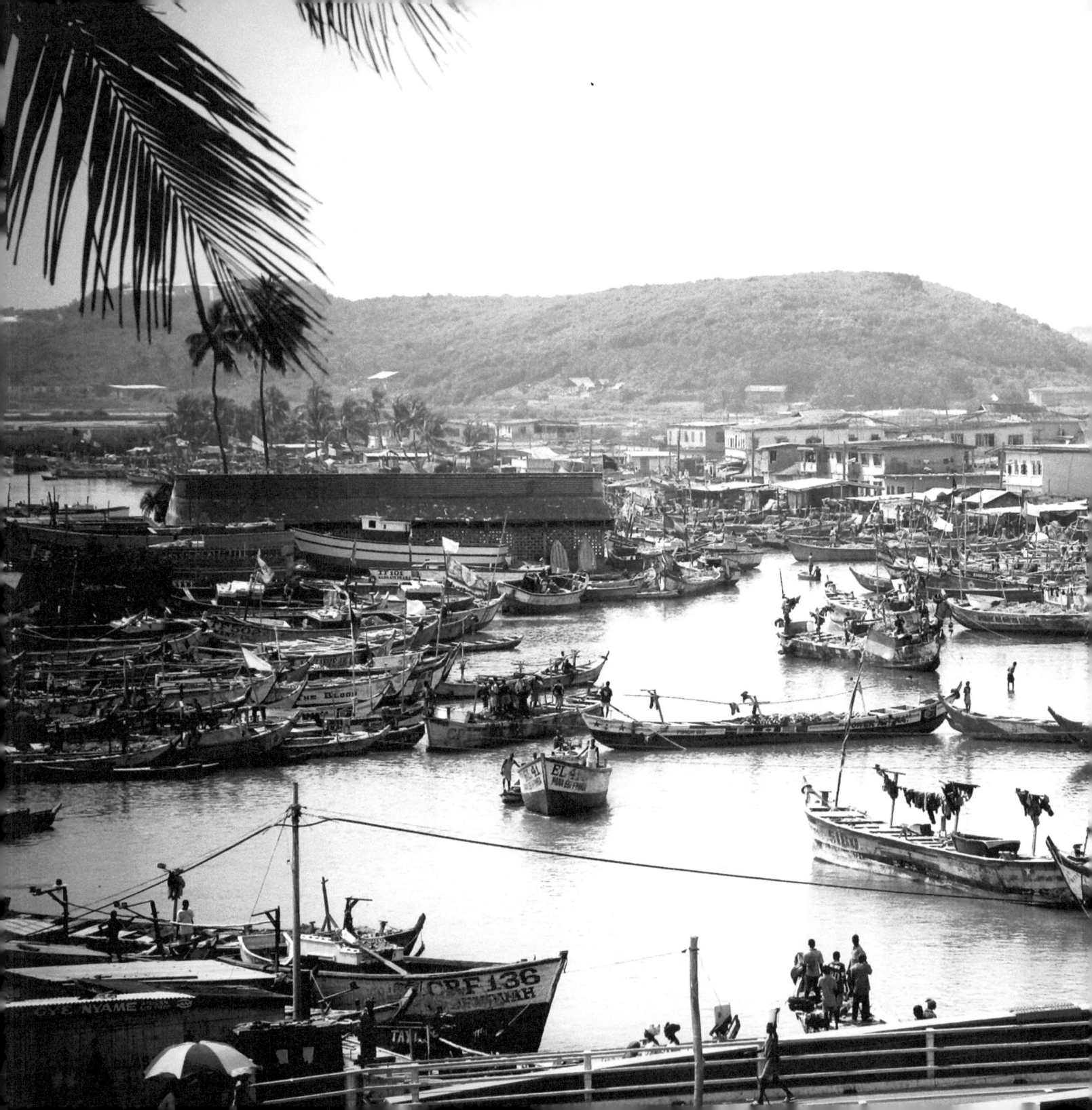

Commute Home

THE WAY IS CONGESTED WITH CHICKENS, CHILDREN, AND SKINNY DOGS. I CAREFULLY WATCH EACH STEP SO AS NOT TO FALL INTO THE FOUL GUTTER. CARS HONK LOUDLY AS THEY SPEED BESIDE ME.

On Thursday night, Renae works two hours late. For the first time I venture back to Elmina on my own after dark. The nearby taxi station stops working around nightfall, when the regular traffic slows down. I walk cautiously toward the market, behind which the main station rests. At night the wide sewage holes blend in with the dark street. I carefully watch each step so as not to fall into the foul gutter. Cars honk loudly as they speed beside me. Children race through the streets. Young kids call out, "Brunie, brunie!" from stone stoops.

Tro tros and taxis run around the market streets, but the taxi station is nowhere within sight. I ask one driver after another for Elmina. They all point toward the same indefinite direction. I walk aimlessly from one busy corner to the next.

A round woman wearing an elaborate black and white dress motions me to come over. She lumbers down from a tro tro that just arrived and indicates for me to follow. "I am going to Elmina. Come," she says in broken English. I follow her silently. In stiff sandals she glides past heaps of rubble, open gutters, and women grilling salty fish along the narrow road. The way is congested with chickens, children, and skinny dogs. A small parking lot is located behind the intricate maze of vendors and broken kiosks. Taxis wait to fill up their cars before making their routes out of the city. The woman motions me to the right, where a man yells out numbers in Fante. I mimick her as she opens the door to a vehicle painted in red and yellow. "You come here," she indicates the parking lot, "or drivers try to take money." She points toward my purse and smiles. Moments later an enthusiastic guy wearing thin-rimmed glasses hops in the front seat. He says he was from the States. His uncles lived in Atlanta and Sacramento. "I am glad we met." he exclaims, "You will come to my house!"

As is customary, the question is posed as a fact of circumstances rather than an invitation. "You are in my country, you will come to my house."

A large man wearing a striped shirt drenched in perspiration crams into the backseat just before we roll out toward Elmina. The men argue in Fante throughout the ride. I squeeze in awkwardly between the woman and the damp man. He hollers toward the driver who continues to look back at us while winding around a busy intersection. His thick arm grows ever moister.

At the Shell Petrol Station, I hop out of the car and run around to the driver window. "It is covered," Atlanta man yells as I reach into my purse, "I got it!"

They think I am a natural at navigating the culture. I must have impressed them with my ability to drink out of a plastic bag.

75

Police Checkpoint

UNLESS THE DRIVER SLIPS A NOTE OF UP TO 10,000 CEDIS, AN OFFICIAL WILL OFTEN TICKET A LARGE AMOUNT THAT MUST BE SETTLED IN COURT.

Chug…chug…chug…chug

At the police checkpoint a man in navy blue motions us to pull to the side. Daniel had stacked more than thirty panels on the top rack. We were officially overloaded. This is a major offense.

To prevent tro tros—public, second hand vans—from over packing to the point of tipping over, it is illegal to surpass a certain weight limit. The exact weight limit is ambiguous, so officials can stop whomever they choose and ignore those who can bribe. The bribe has become a ritual part of the checkpoint process. Unless the driver slips a note of up to 10,000 cedis, an official will often issue a ticket that must be settled in court. Most Ghanaians cannot afford the high fee, nor the time to settle the matter. Consequently, their licenses are revoked. Officials collect bribes from taxis and tro tros multiple times a day. They strip the drivers of their wages, sometimes for no legitimate reason.

Teresa hands Daniel a note for 10,000 cedis. He hops out of the jeep, ramming his leg against the side, which causes a wound. The officer, looking disgusted as Daniel sops up blood with a dirty rag, forces Daniel to open the front hood and check the break fluid. Daniel limps back to the driver's seat and hands him the money. The officer rants in Fante and then motions us on. Daniel smiles as the three of us look forward in shock. He waves to a row of officers in identical blue uniforms sitting on the opposite side of the road.

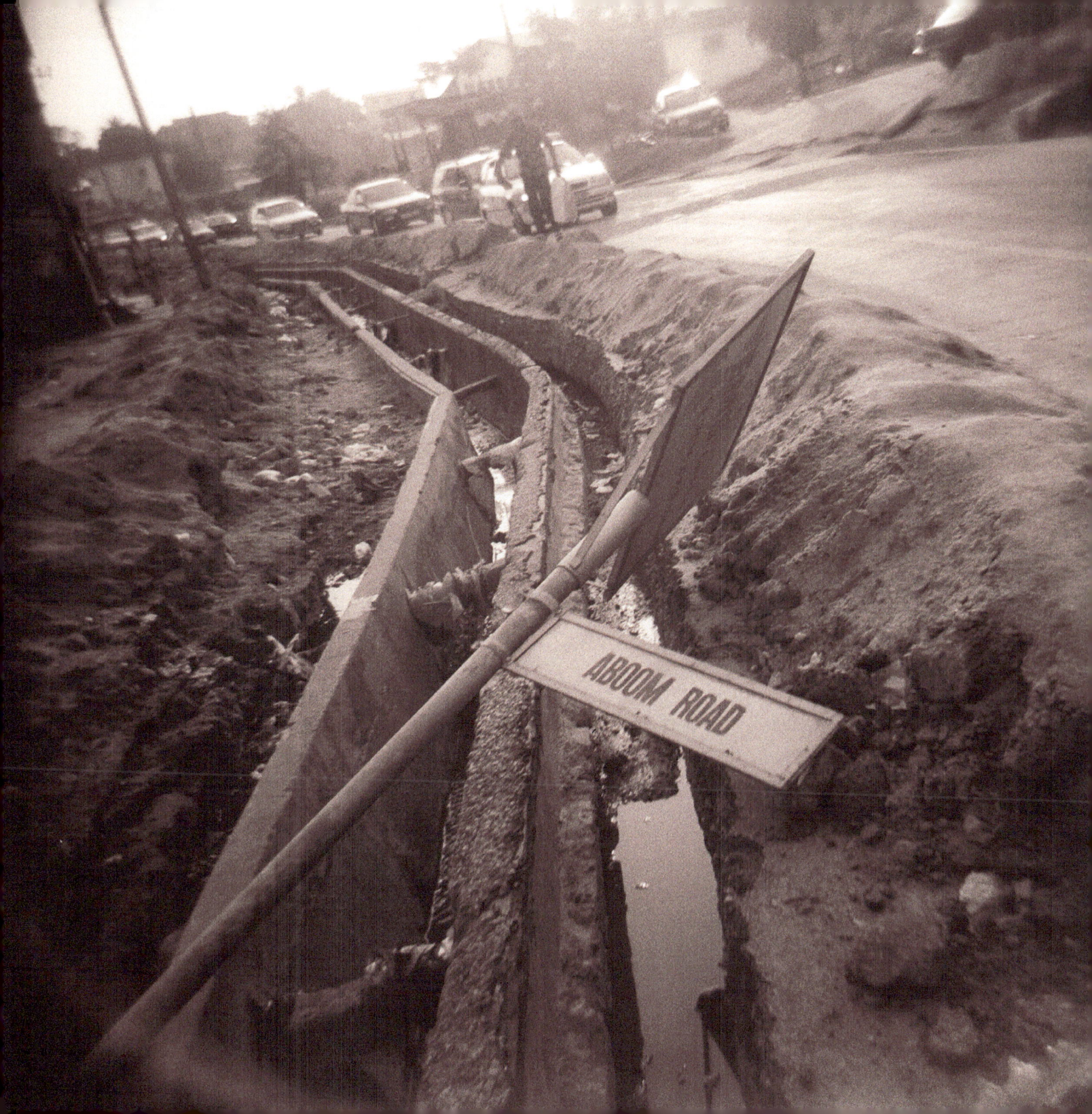

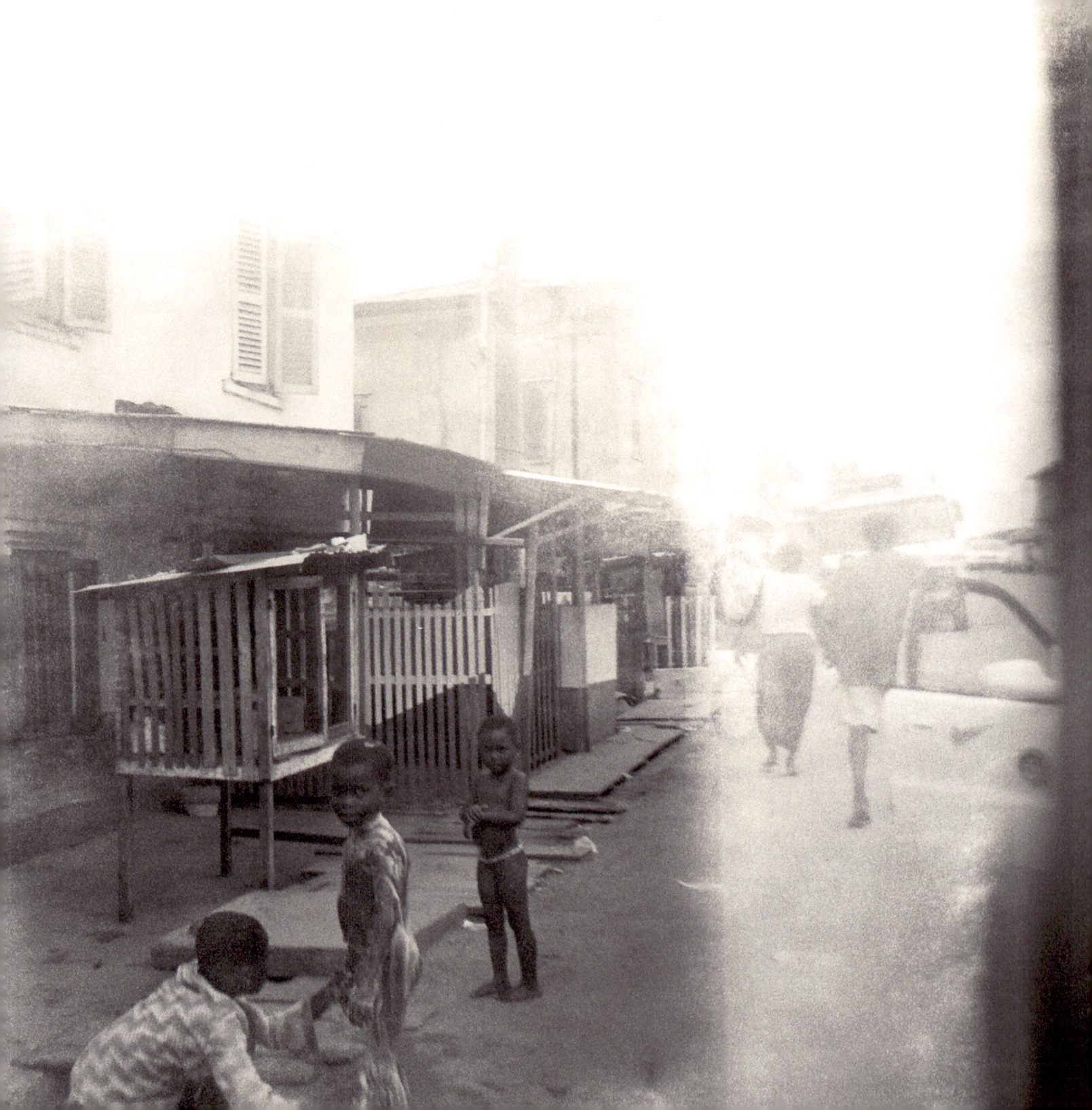

Eeee-yunta, eeee-yunta, eeee-yunta…

Eighteen months old, a boy drinks
from his mother's breast. She wears a
vibrant dress of ruby red with amber
circles.
A spot of white pigment decorates his
forehead.

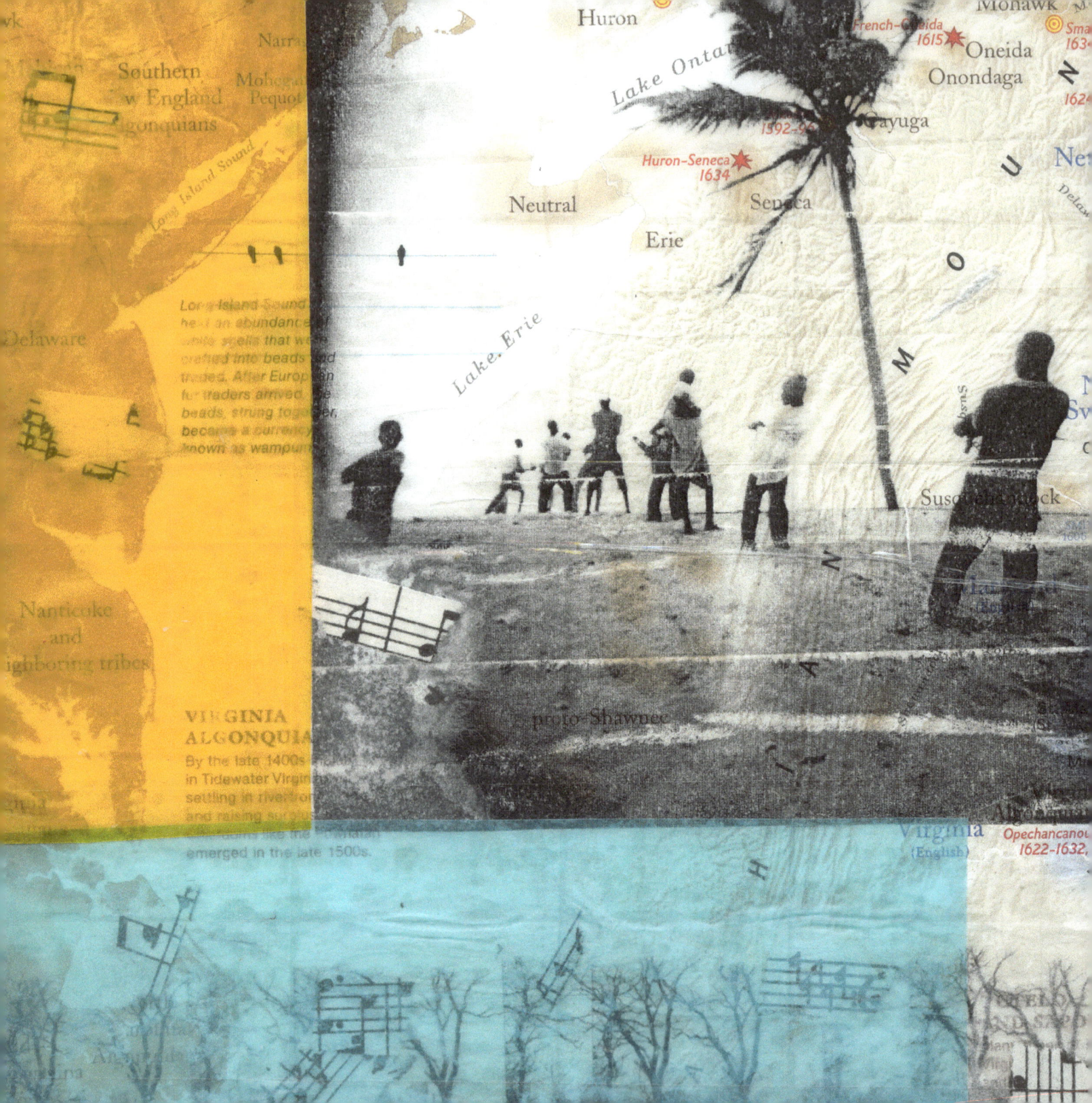

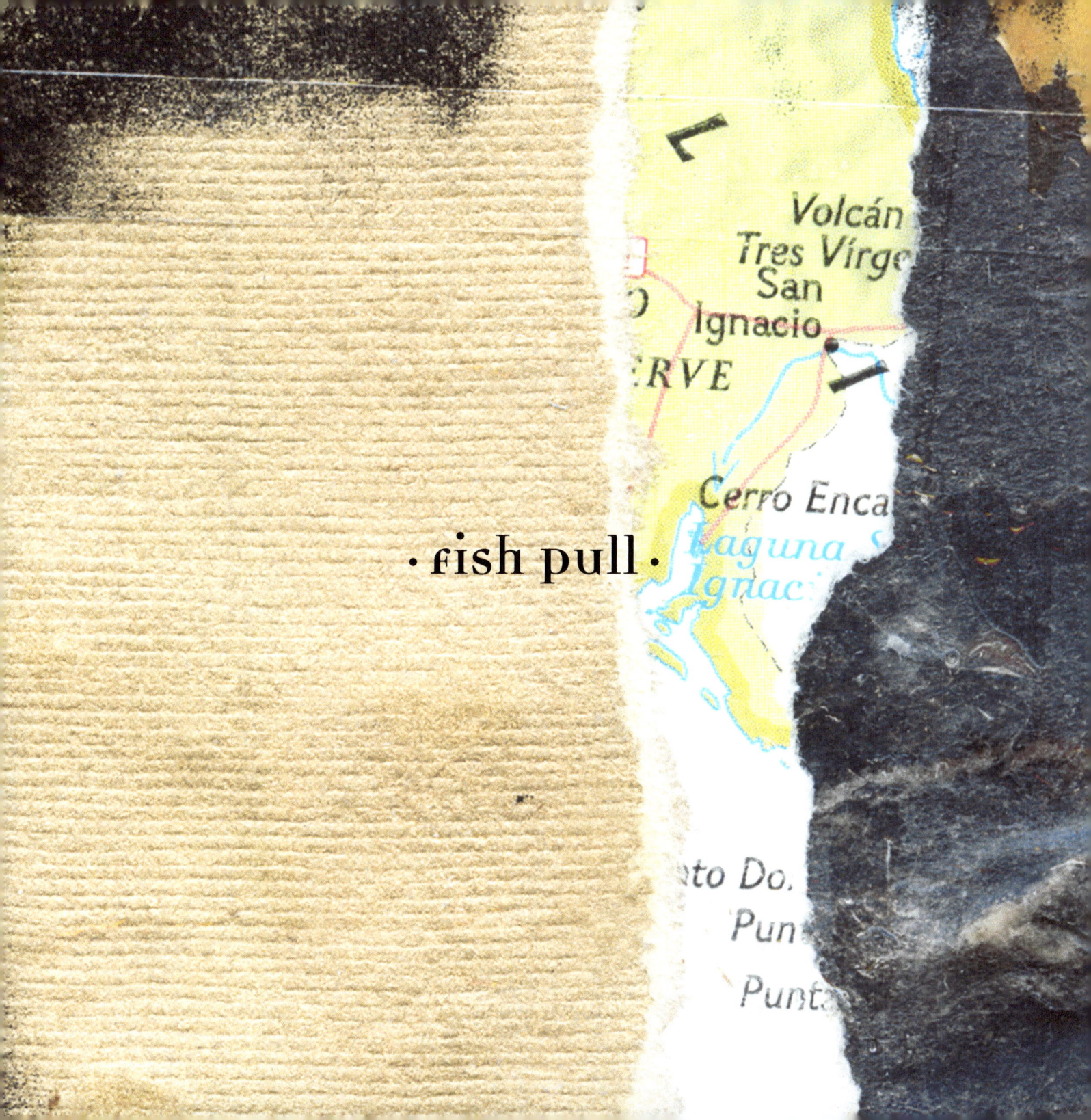

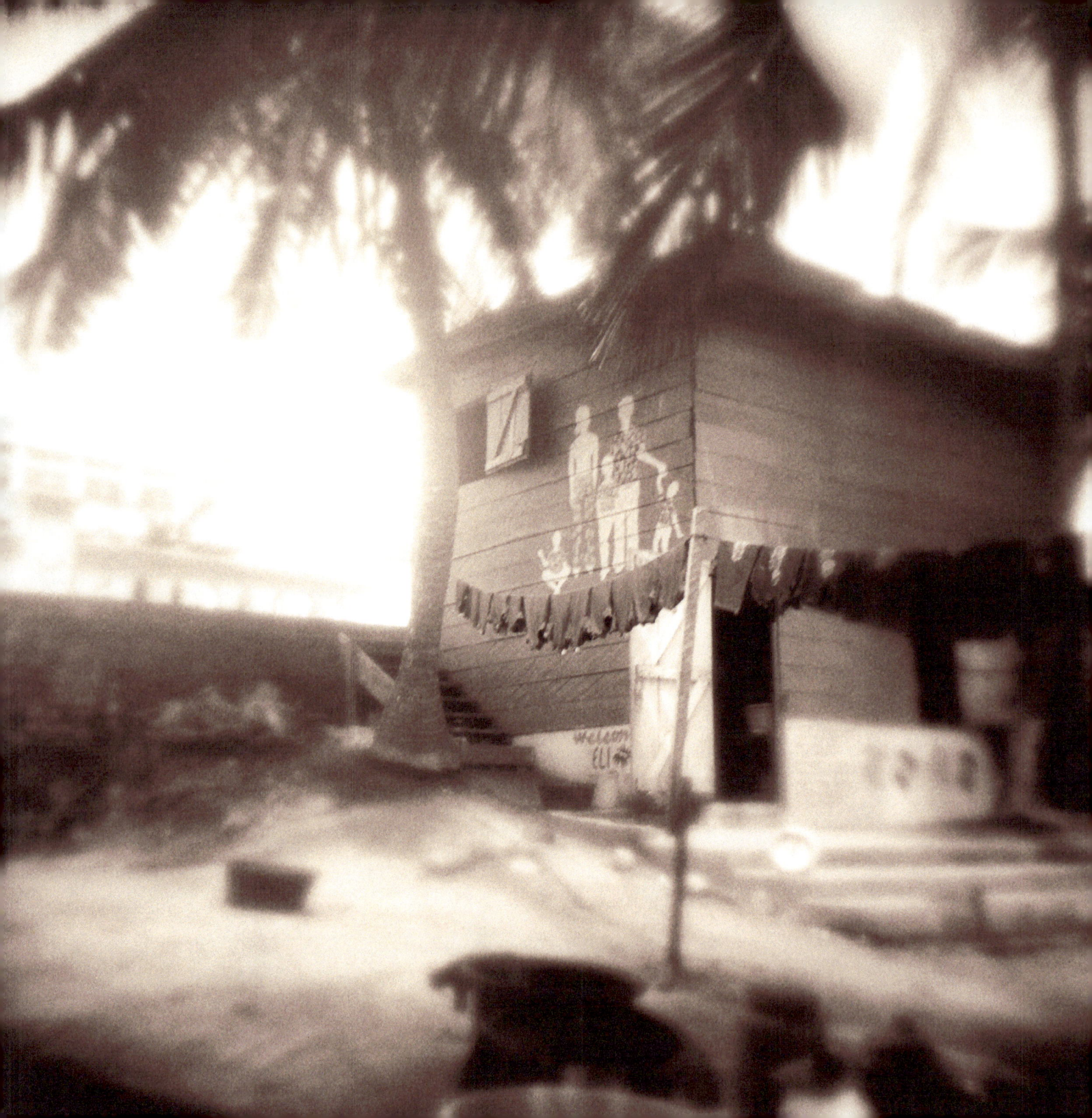

A boy in black tattered pants does
acrobatics beside the sea. In a neat line,
he flips back gracefully, waving his arms
in crazy motion to the imaginary crowd.
He draws a circle in the sand with his
finger and steps inside.

Flip.

He twirls his body back in the air and
lands directly inside the circle. For an
hour he whirls his limbs in the air,
pirouettes, and poses.

*Ding ding...... ding ding...... ding......
ding...... ding ding ding.*

The scent of roasted plantains trickles into
the café.

Fishing...A Week in a Day

At the tip of Moree Island, The Village of Ahwiado sits between a lagoon and the ocean. A cluster of mud huts with palm-thatched roofs sleeps beneath a cover of smoky haze.

Amy and I walk on soft sand for thirty minutes before reaching the mark on Matilda's hand-scrawled map. People pile on shore, sifting through nets of shiny, silver fish. Oddly, nobody seems to acknowledge us, two white girls wandering around aimlessly toward the village.

The sun will set in an hour. My old mobile phone fails to work on the beach, and nobody we ask recognizes the name Renae. After a mile walk through soft sand with a bruised leg from a rocky fall, I refuse to acknowledge that we are lost.

Wilson appears moments later. He leads us to an open courtyard enclosed in a palm-thatched fence. The center consists of five mud huts and a wide area for smoking fish. He directs us to a bench beneath a palm awning, and introduces us to a large-boned woman named Agnes, and to Robert, another young village leader. Wilson is to serve as our translator, conversationalist, and wannabe ladies' man.

Renae's Ewe (tribal) name is Abayaa because she was born on a Thursday.

Abayaa is a celebrity in the small Ewe fishing village. "Abayaa," Wilson says nobly, "brought us fresh water."

For more than two years Renae lived on the island as a Peace Corps volunteer. During that time, she raised money for the task of installing a pipe and faucet in the village that furnished it with fresh water. With the help of contractors, engineers, and many drunken Ewe fishermen, she extended her stay to manage the long project. A majority of the work took place on Tuesday, the one day the fishermen do not fish. Naturally, Monday became drinking night.

In six months, the men dug the long hole to make a cradle for the pipe. Once the project was complete, women no longer had to walk with heavy bowls on their heads down a long trail to the stream to collect water. The village refers to Renae as the queen mother.

On a wood board beside the public faucet, the community carved THANK YOU ABAYAA JUNE '94

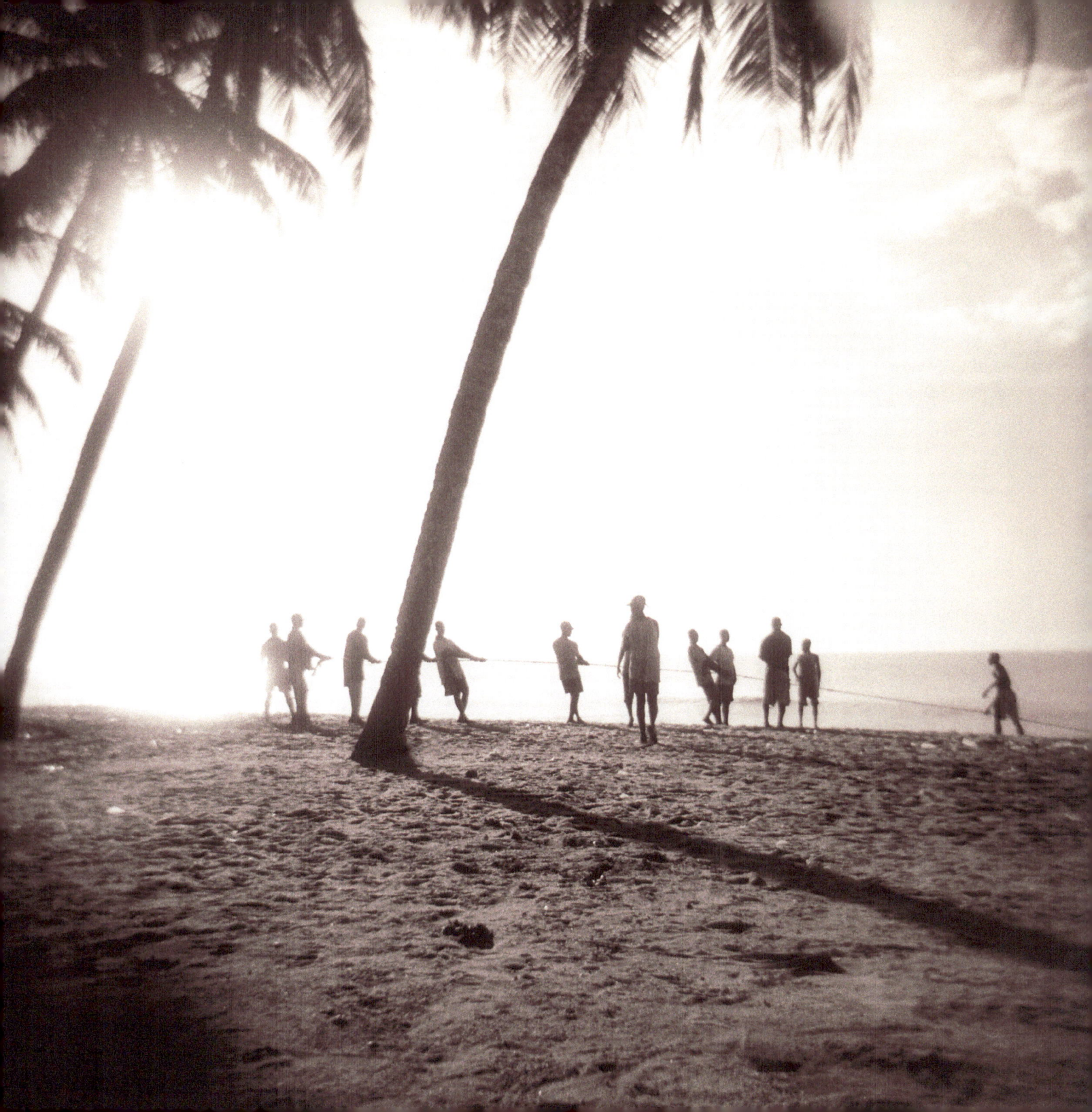

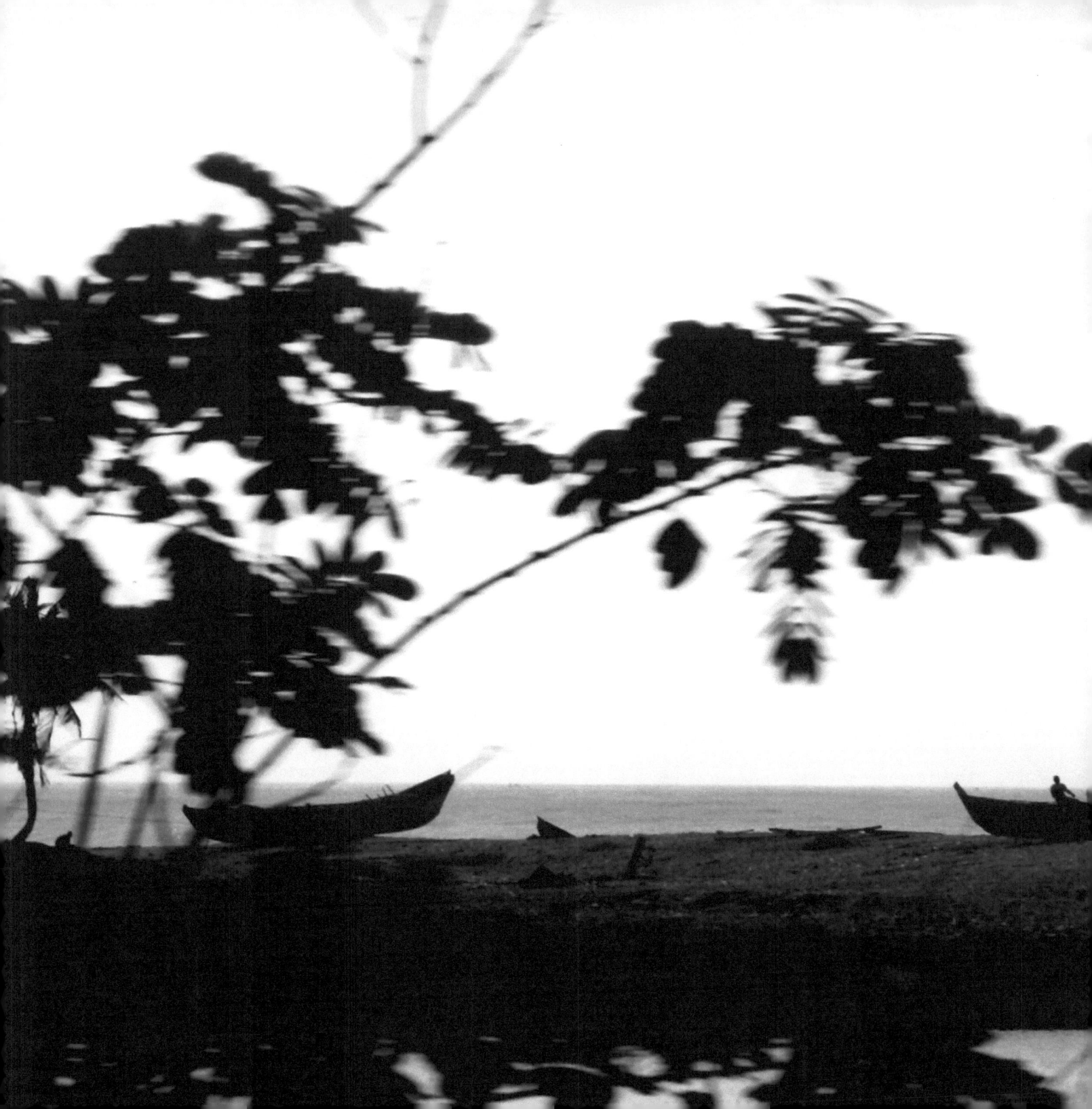

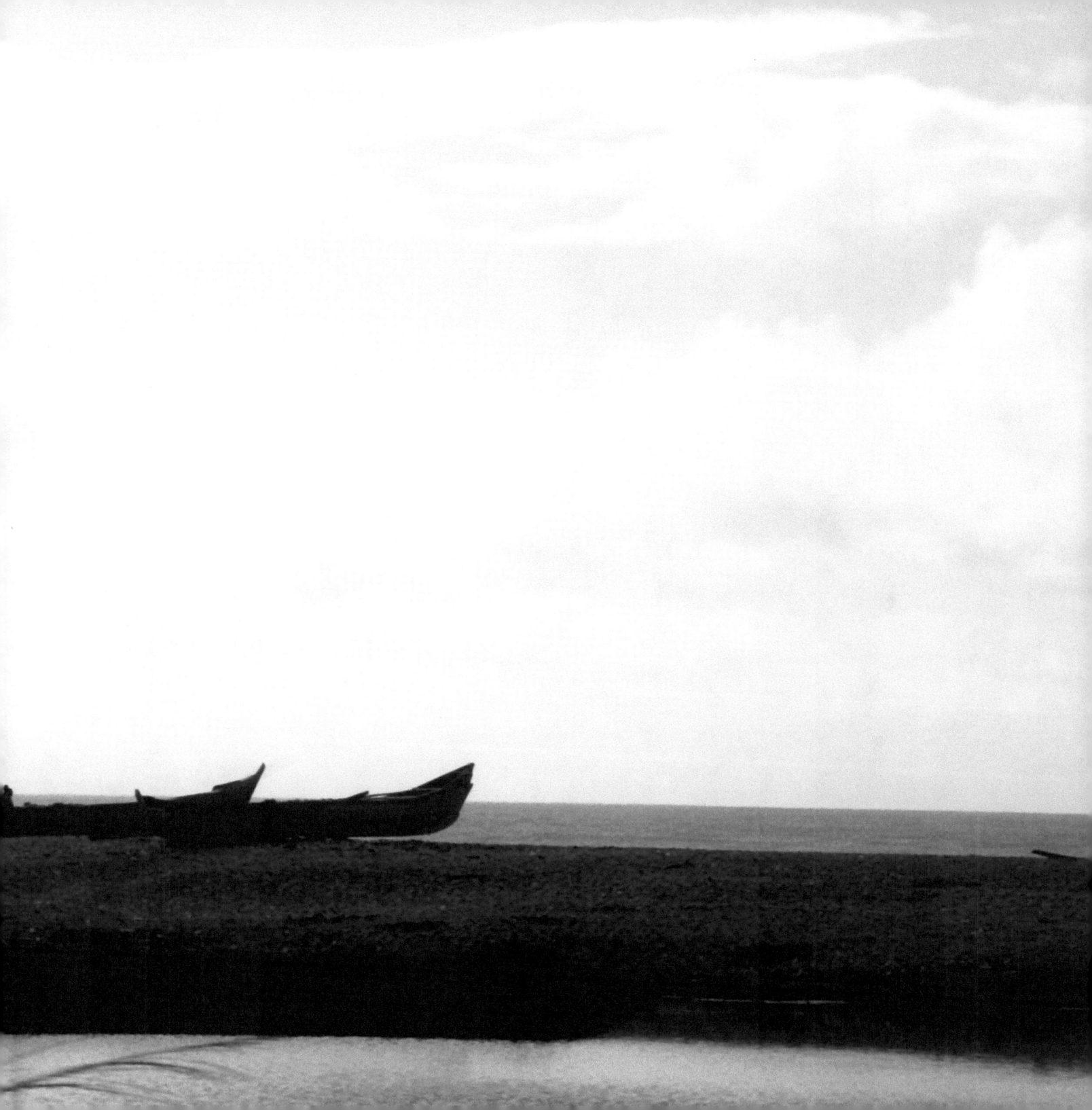

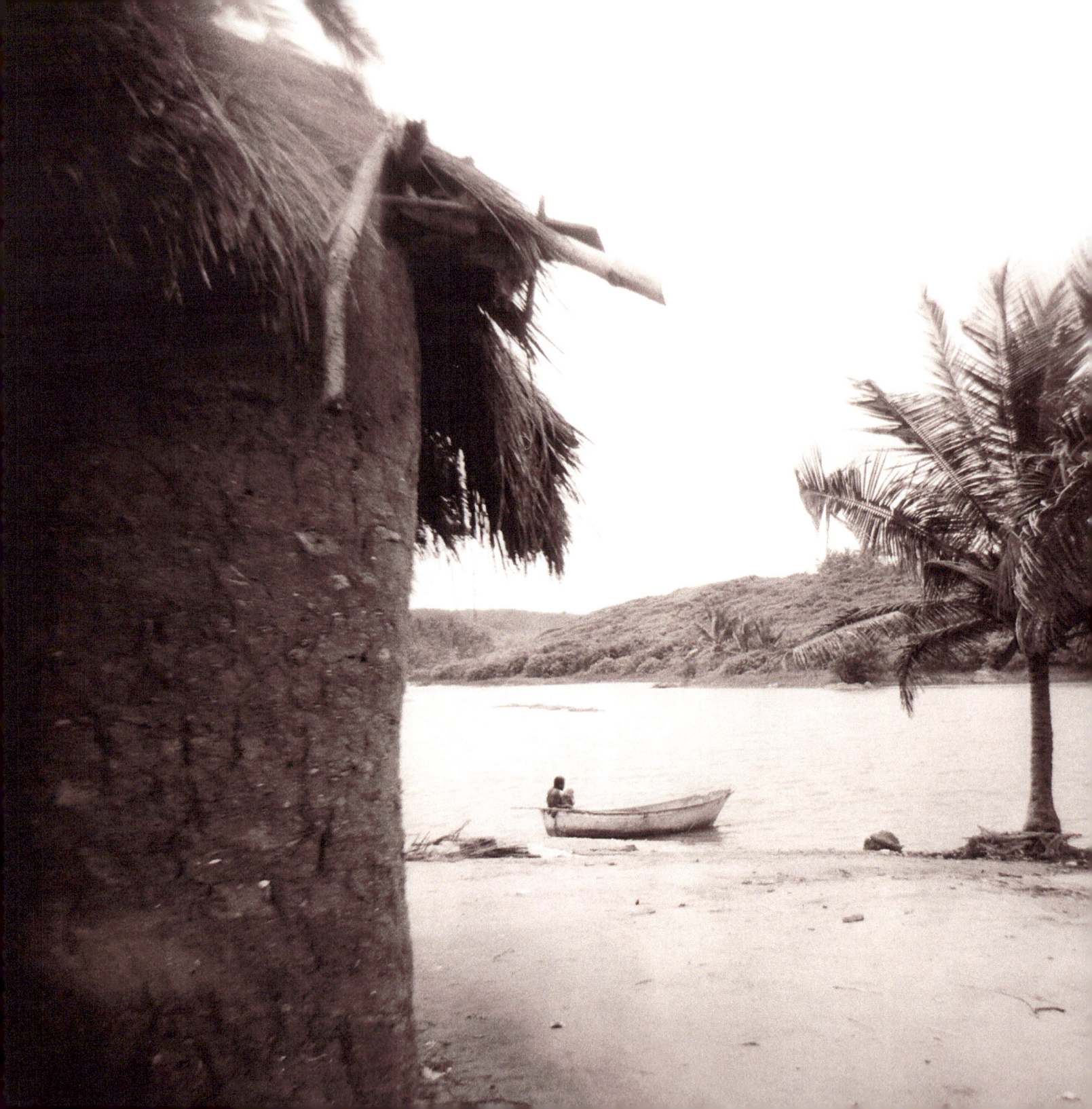

It is difficult to explain the smell of a rainy night.

It is the combination of fresh baked bread…and the cloth towel under which it has been culturing for days.

The first fishing boat left at 4am to drop the nets. Amy and I sit on the shore until the second boat sets out just after 10am. A single line of men play tug-of-war with the ocean, chanting with each pull…

Eee-yaaah…… eeee-yahhhh…
eee-yunta……Eeee-yuntaaaaaa.

The divide between the educated and the uneducated in the Ewe tribe becomes quite apparent to us. Young guys on break from university introduce themselves articulately. Old men with bread and porridge lodged in crooked teeth garble a welcome in broken English. They make hopeful demands. "You will give us money!?"

Robert presents us to a group of male elders, who meet in a concrete cove. They all own fishing nets, and are thus considered the community leaders. He lengthens our brief thanks into a long speech spoken in rapid Ewe. The men seem to approve. They nod their heads solemnly.

The Men of the Ewe

IN THE PURPLE GLOW, WOMEN START SWEEPING WITH THIN-STICK BROOMS. NEAT LINES STENCIL INTO THE SAND LIKE A ZEN GARDEN.

fish pull

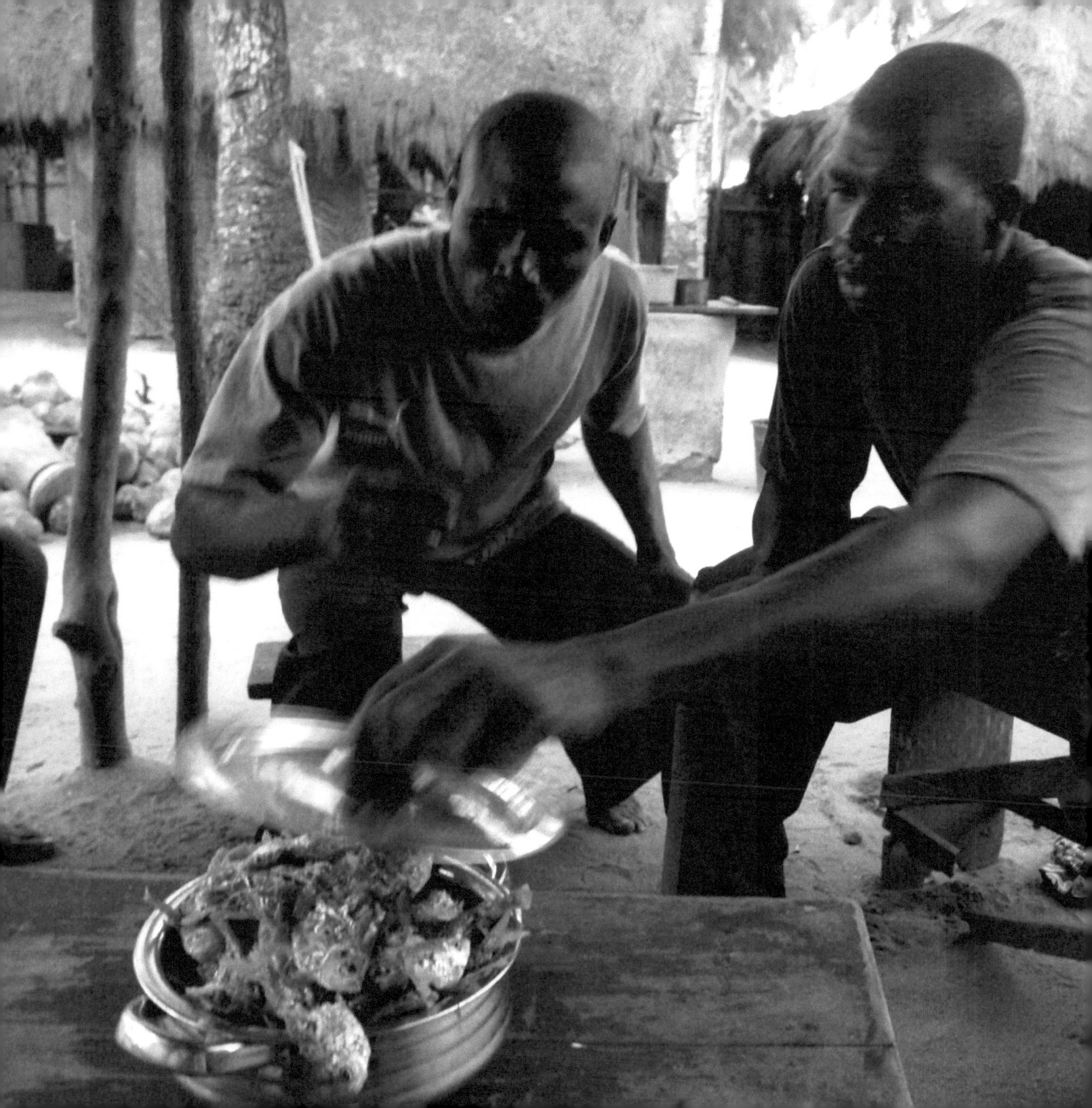

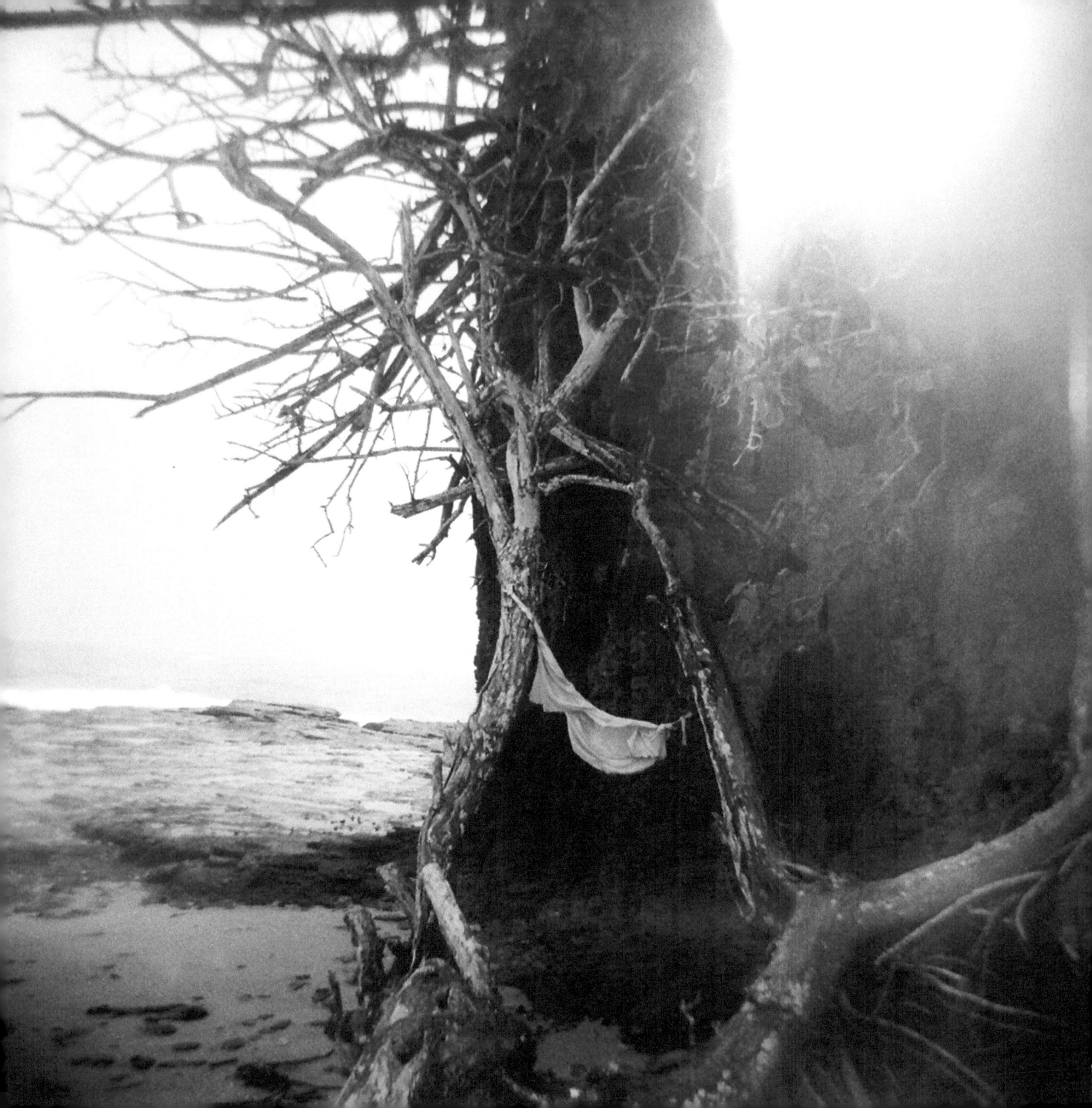

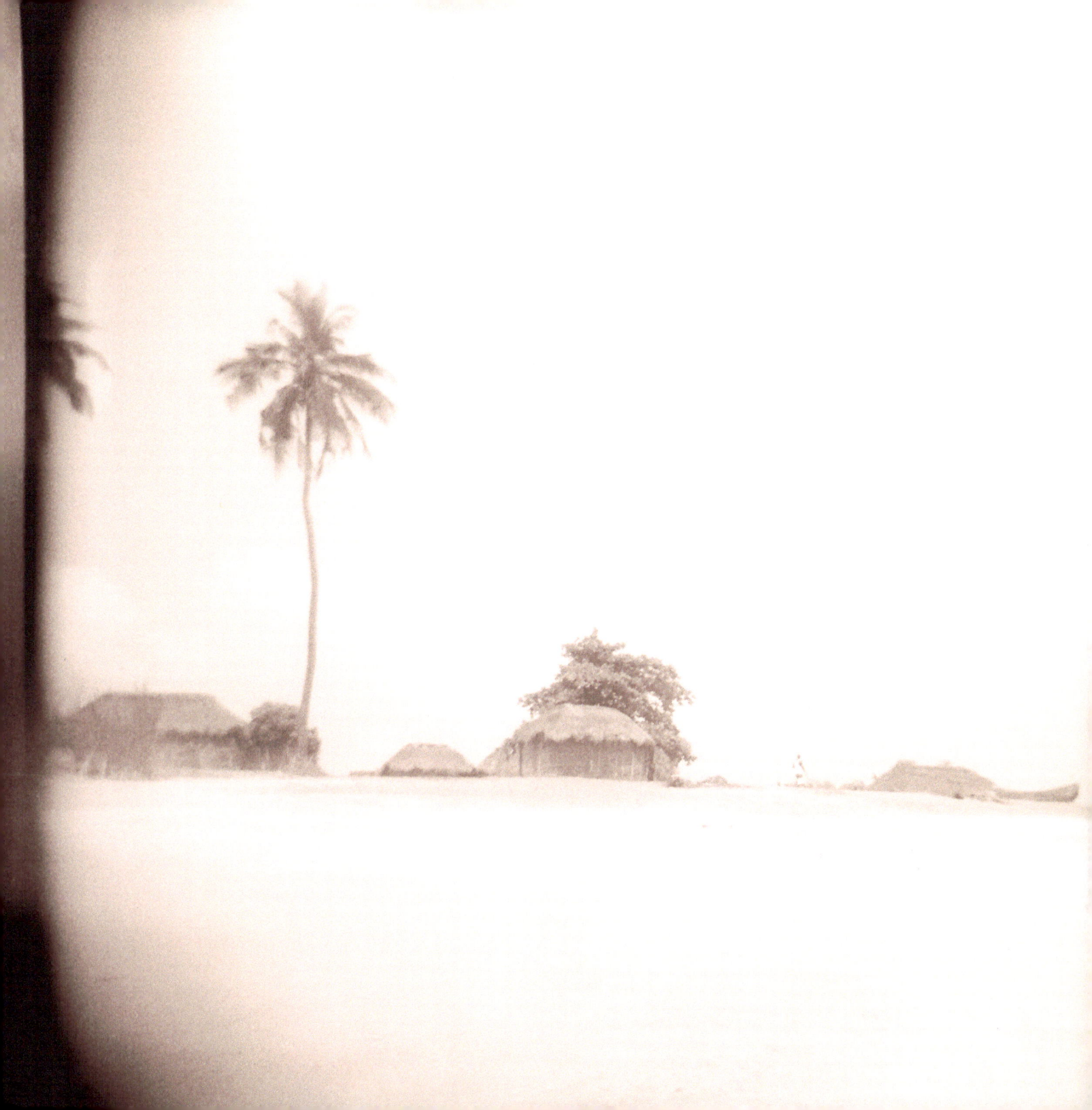

Afternoon
Fishing Boat

THE MEN GRAB HEAVY
WOOD OARS AND ROW LIKE
MACHINES AS WE PLOUGH
INTO BREAKING WAVES.
THE BOAT'S EDGE DIPS
SEVERELY TO THE SIDE.

Hurry, hurry, hurry…

At 10am, the second fishing boat is ready to drop the nets. A striking man named George introduces himself as my guide. He has a warm smile and chiseled arms. I race after him toward a long wooden boat. He grips a plastic bag that holds my clunky camera with his teeth.

"Jump in!"

Men surround the boat. They hold it in place as I hoist up my white linen skirt and climb over the high side. I sit on a blue net that is tangled between eight parallel boards.

"Sit in the middle!"

Ten men fly into the boat. George plops down beside me in the middle of the show. The sides rock dangerously. Waves crash and rumble toward us. The men grab heavy wooden oars and row like machines as we plough into breaking waves. The boat's edge dips severely to the side. Water streams into the center as we rock back and forth, back and forth... my knuckles are white. I grab onto the seat and rest my weight on George. He wears a white t-shirt cut at the shoulders. On his shirt, a long-haired woman in an antique French print smiles at me.

An old man starts an engine wrapped in purple batik. Once we pass the waves, the boat glides deeper into the water.

Black smoke fumes from the old motor. From the distance, I can see Cape Coast castle, where white men first transported slaves. Beside me, a man wearing a red wool hat scoops out water. Four men swing toward the front of the boat, using my shoulder as a crutch. They pull green fishing nets up from the water. George explains their motives, but I can barely listen…. something about concrete in the nets. The boat nearly tips. They yank the nets up over the edge. Small fish whip around the wire. A vein bulges from the neck of a man wearing a blue Adidas top.

"Are you scared?" George asks calmly. Somehow I am not.

The men laugh and banter in Ewe. A crewman lifts his oar above his head to signal men on shore to pull the nets. Identical thin boats pass by, carrying much fewer men. They wave and holler.

"Are they wondering why there is a little white girl in your boat?"

"They are greeting you!"

As they prepare to drop the net, the fishermen rush me to the front. George and his brother sit closely beside me. We face the entire crew. The men find this amusing, joking in rhythmic gibberish.

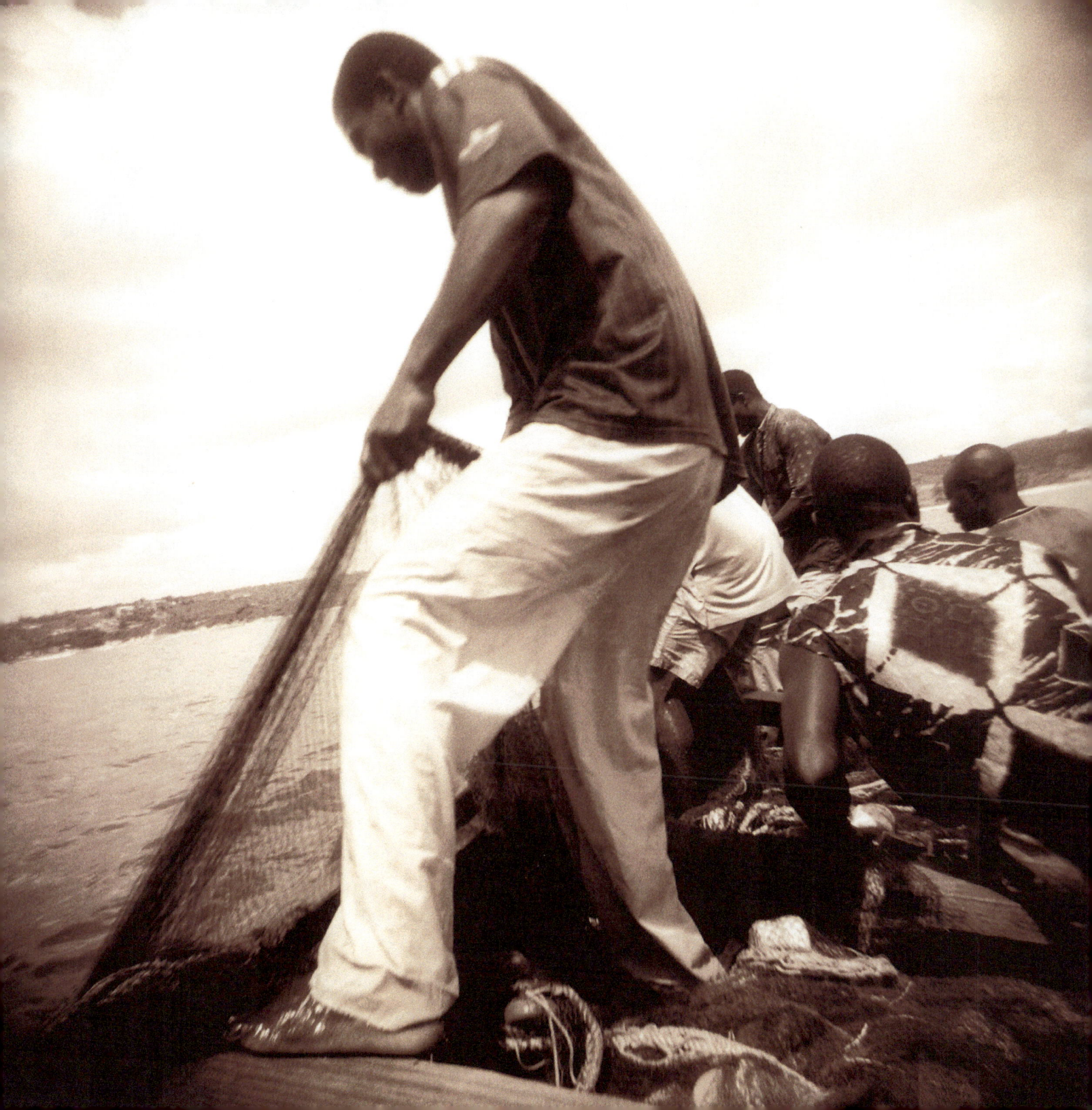

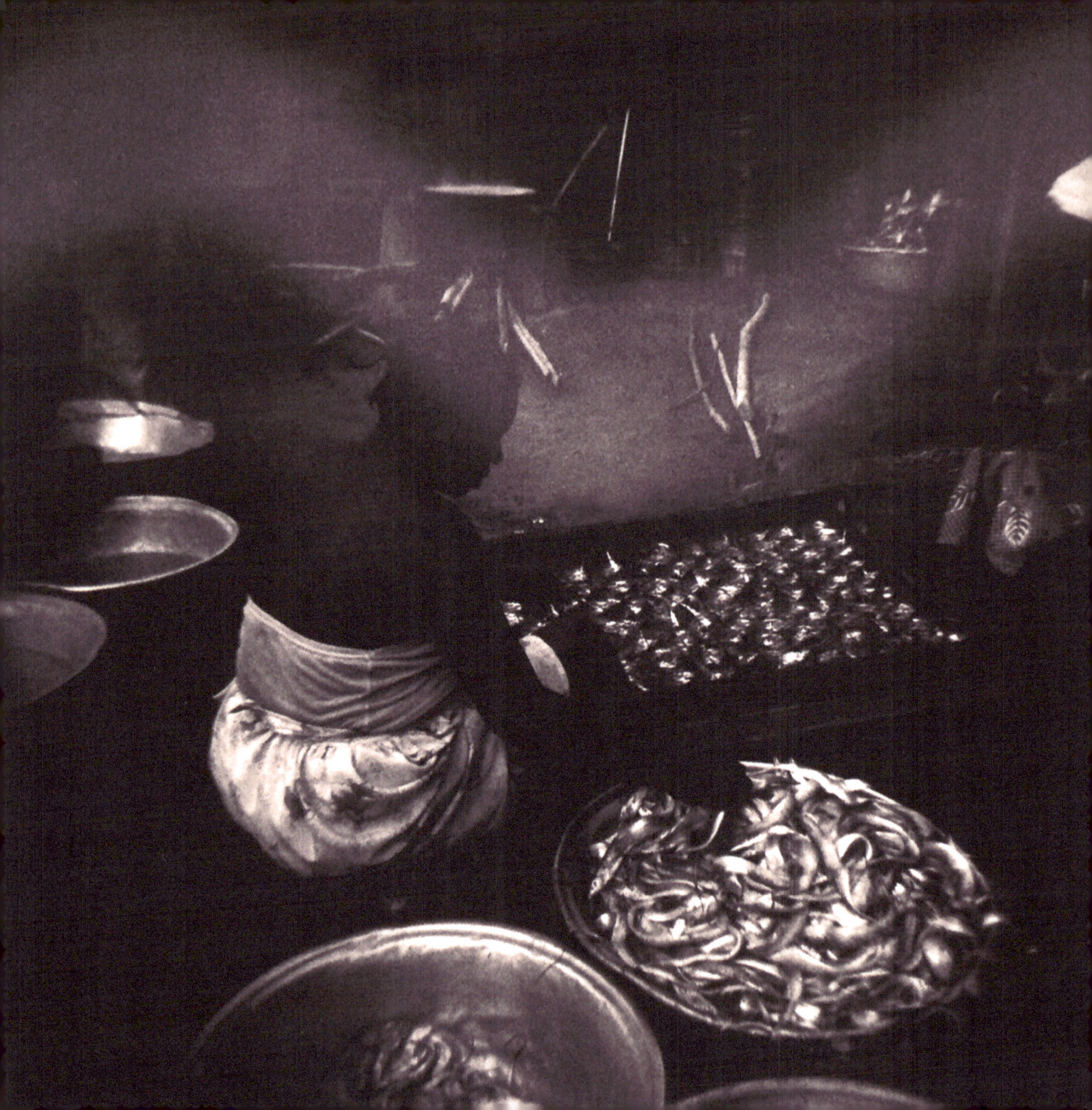

Farther into the ocean, long blue nets dive quickly into the sea. The sides of the boat rock drastically down. George places his hands under my arms and re-positions me like an infant. The rope my feet are resting on whips into the water after the net. A man in green mesh ties the end of another piece of rope to a hot pink anchor and flings it into the water. Again, they raise the oars to signal a second pull. I balance my feet on a bundle of oars. The boat inches toward shore.

"Do you know how to swim?" Men jump out of the boat and swim to shore.

"Uh, yeah. Now?"

"No, no. Wait."

We move to the middle of the boat. Only six men remain. "Are you sure you can swim this far?" The men look worried.

"Yeah!" The distance does not appear that far, but the boat seems to be moving further away from the sand.

"The boat must go back to sea. Can you surely swim?"

"Yes!"

"OK"

"Now?!!"

"No, no. Wait." George sits calmly.

"Ok, let's go."

"Now??!!" I don't believe him. I jump out before I have time to consider the actual distance.

Water gushes into my mouth. The salt stings my throat. I start swimming freestyle. The water feels refreshing and cool, but the current is much stronger than it appears. I have not swum freestyle in five years. The man in green mesh swims behind me. Like George had before, he carries my camera in a plastic bag with his teeth.

"Go! Go! Go!" George catches up to me in seconds. Like a football coach he screams, "Go! Go! Go!"

He swims effortlessly alongside me, laughing and encouraging. I gulp seawater. The weight of my skirt drags me down. The shore seems miles away, and then in minutes, it is close. My arms become gummy. I turn onto my back and kick.

"You are good!"

Water fills my nose. I roll around and force my arms to move. George grabs me for a moment and then I feel the sand beneath my feet. A wave crashes over my head. I swallow more water and jump to my feet again.

Another wave, down, back up, and we are on shore. A string of men line the beach up to the village.

I follow George up to the courtyard like a numb, excited puppy. A bucket bath waits for me in a roofless washroom. Amy arrives soon after. Robert has sailed her around peacefully on the lagoon.

WATER FILLS MY NOSE. I ROLL AROUND AND FORCE MY ARMS TO MOVE. GEORGE GRABS ME FOR A MOMENT AND THEN I FEEL THE SAND BENEATH MY FEET. A WAVE CRASHES OVER MY HEAD.

97

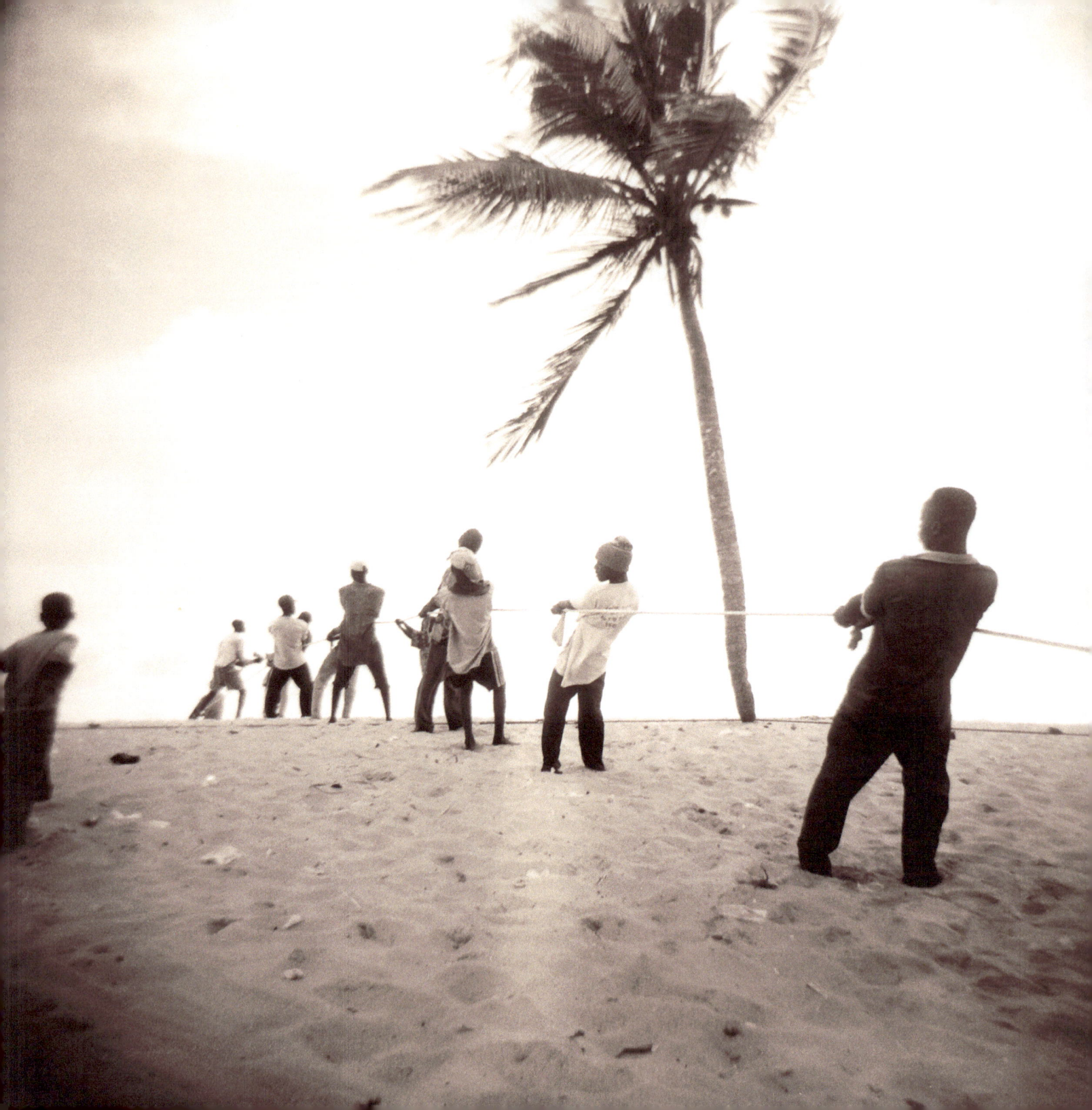

Bummm, buh, bummm, buh, commmme
back to me......

come back, come back, come back to me......

......ohhhh sweetheart, come back to me....

fish pull

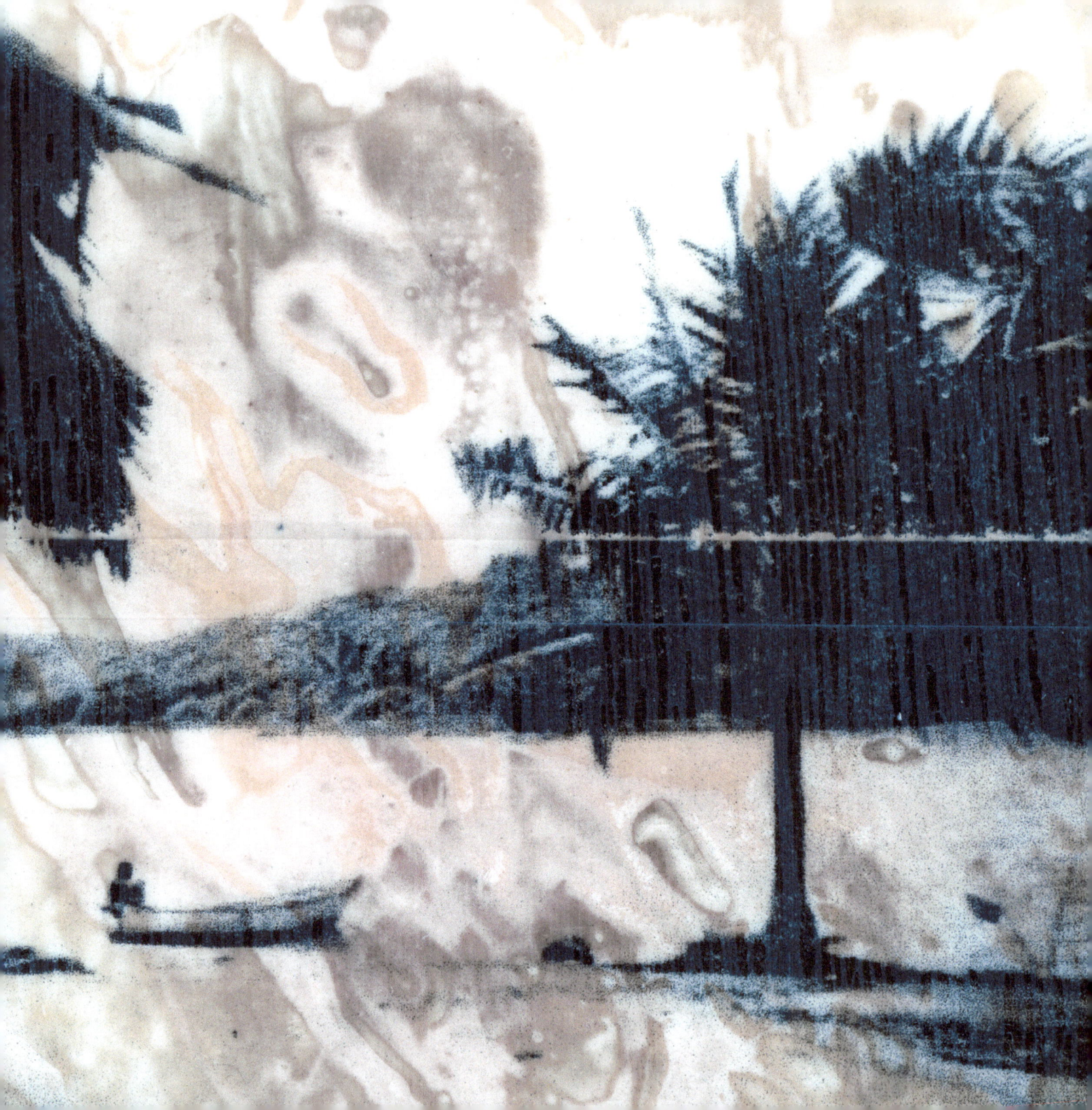

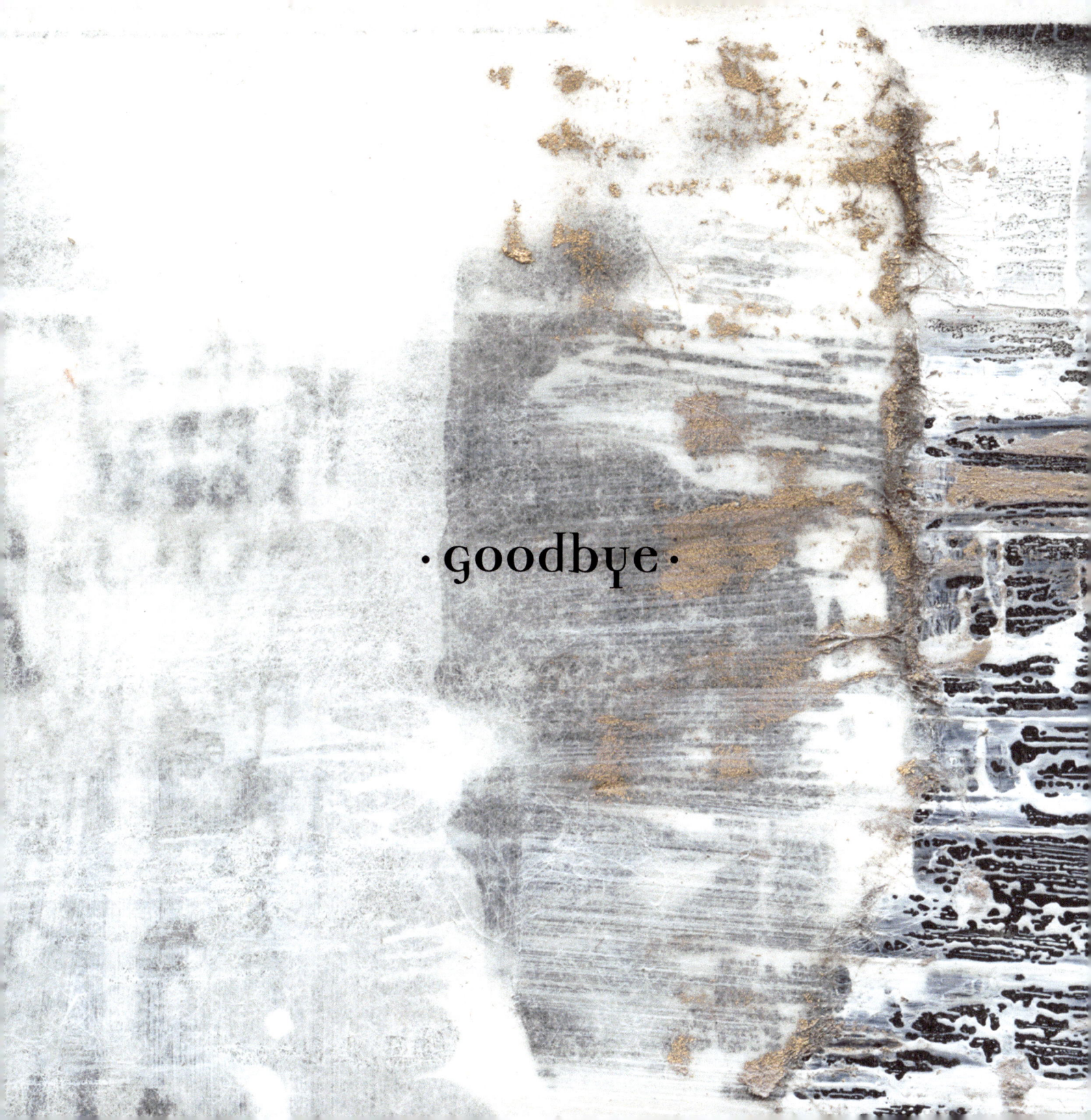

Krobo Episodes

WE EAT DINNER IN KOKROKO. THE WAITRESS INTRODUCES HERSELF AS BELLA, AND INFORMS ME SHE IS OUT OF TONIC WATER AND ACCOMMODATION.

We eat dinner in the dining room of Kokroko, the only guesthouse in town. Its owner is Nancy, an obese woman who wears baby pink frills and high heels. A polite girl with a soft voice works in the restaurant that resembles a religious retirement facility. Fake rosy flowers are placed in large vases on and around wood tables that encircle a pink room. A large balloon declaring "Happy Birthday" floats in the corner. A landscape painted on wood panels decorates the wall beside depictions of Christ and Mary, plated in fake gold.

Joseph, a lanky bald man, arrives minutes later and drives me to a second site. He tours me around a large, dark house while a small group of locals follow. The first two rooms have old double beds and dingy yellow walls. A ceiling fan hangs overhead. The second room features a neon pink tiled bathroom. The door to the third room highlights Christ on the cross, carved expressively into the wood. A huge roach dashes down the hallway.

"What is that?!" screams Renae.

"Oh!" Joseph stomps on it with his green flip-flop. "Where did that come from?!"

I opt for the second room with the ceiling fan and poppy pink bathroom.

"What is the price of the room?" Renae demands.

"100,000 cedi for all rooms!" Joseph swings his finger toward all the rooms in a circular motion.

"The same price for all rooms? Even for that little room?" Renae points to my tiny double.

"Oh, no, 150,000 for the big room!"

"You just said 100,000 for all the rooms!" Renae mimics his pointing motion.

"Uh, no, 150,000 for big room, 100,000 for rest of rooms."

"Ohhh, I see. Bigger numbers this time," Renae kids around with the men. "I'm afraid to ask a third time."

The room erupts in confused laughter.

"I like you!" He announces.

Renae imitates the line of a popular Ghanaian dance song. "I like you, but I love somebody else… I like you, but I love somebody else." She shakes her hips and darts her fingers in the air. The rest of the room follows in motion, pointing their fingers in the air and dancing in place.

Joseph insists I sign his guest book and send the payment back with Renae. I sign TWEETY in capital letters and date it SOMEDAY.

"Good!"

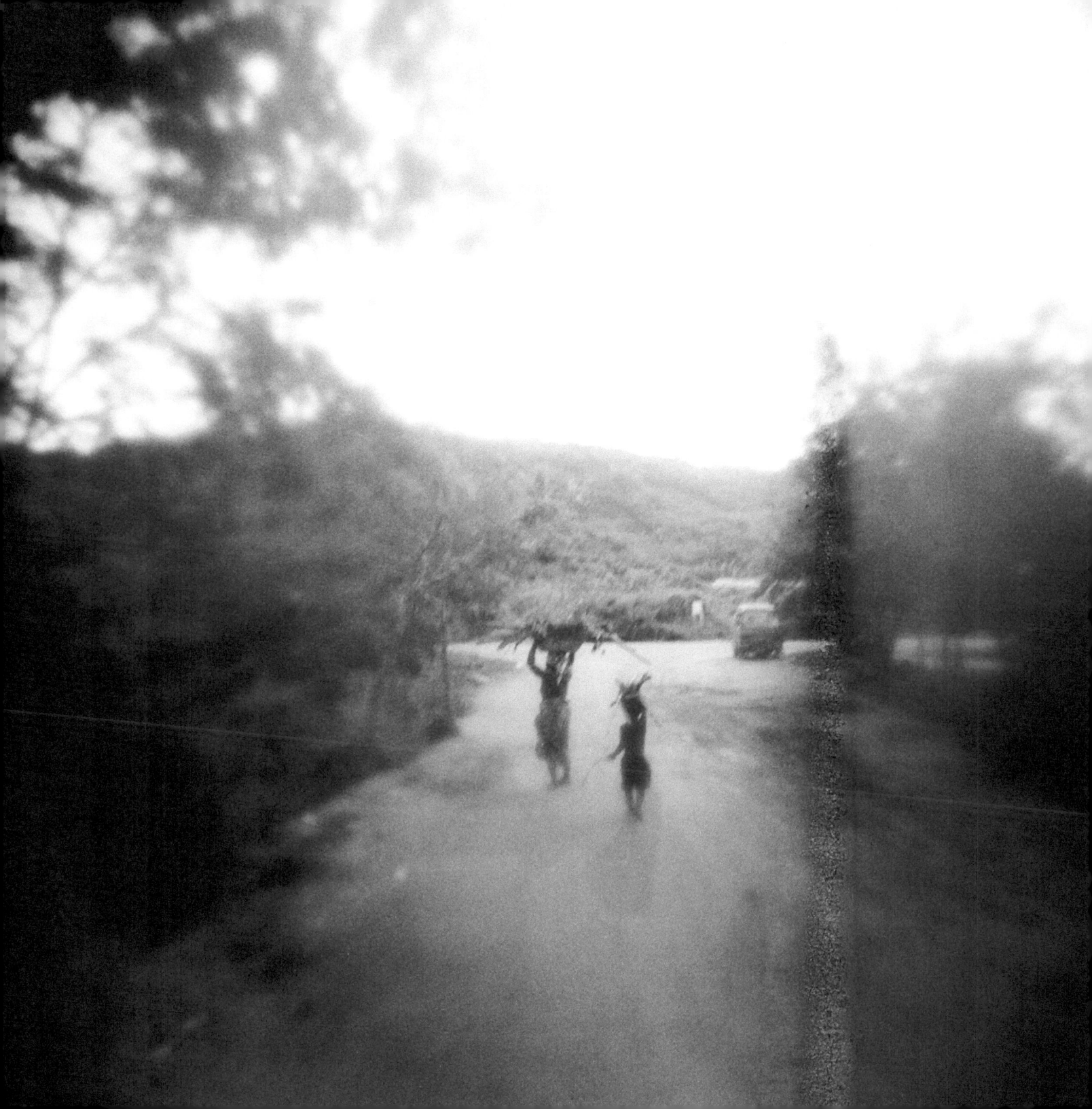

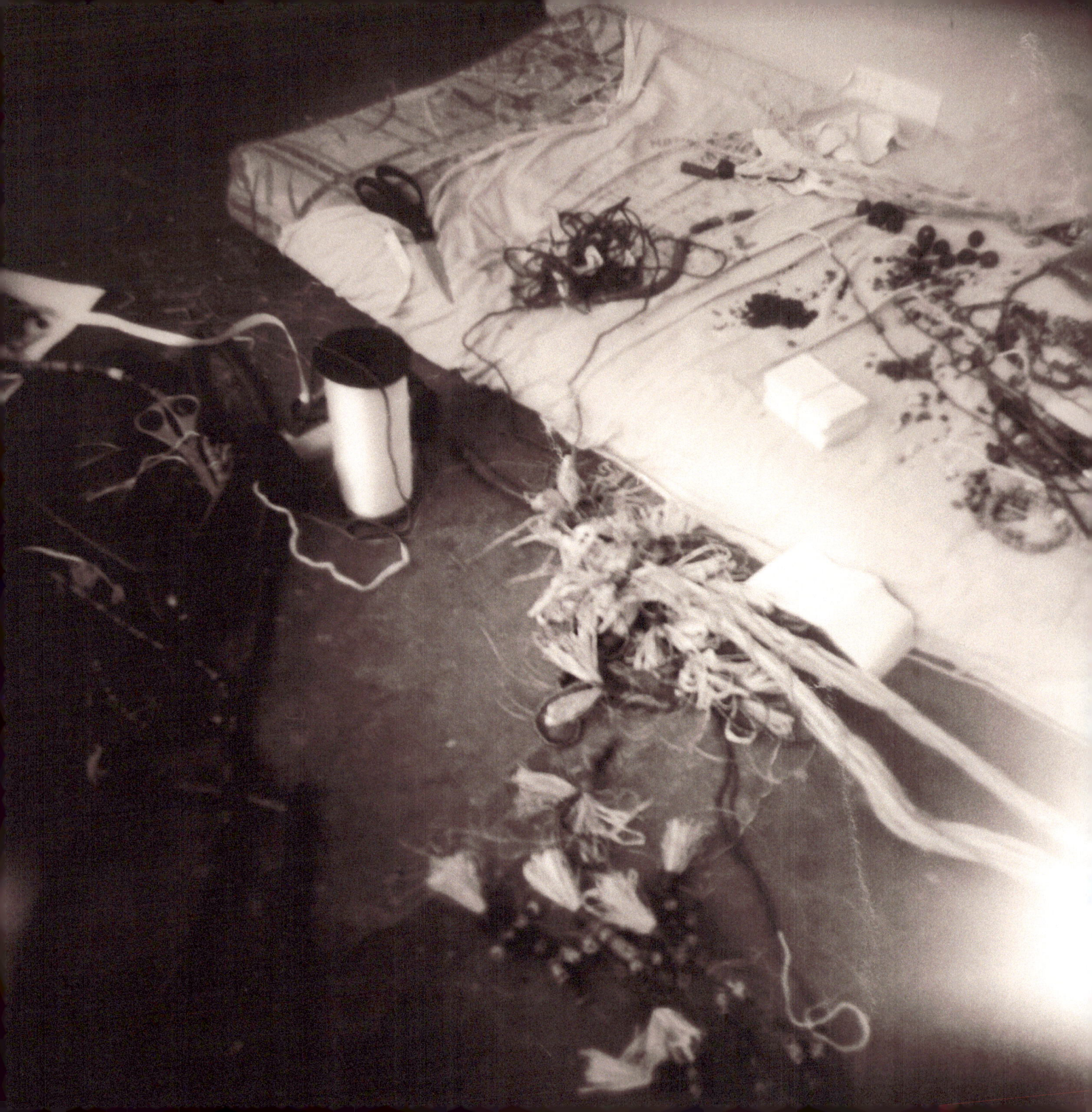

Ophelia Arthur

"When are you leaving?" Kukuwa sits in the kitchen and rests her head on her thin, ebony arms.

"Tuesday!"

"Oh! This Tuesday?!"

"Yeah."

"Will you come back?"

"I hope so. I'm not ready to leave."

"Oh," She giggles. Kukuwa is twenty-one. She started working as a live-in housekeeper for Renae two years ago. Kukuwa now makes more than men and women with a college degree. A past volunteer showed her how to make beaded spirit dolls for Global Mamas. The dolls are now one of the most popular items. Renae ships out thousands of spirits a month. "I have to tell you something."

"Yeah?" I lean against the counter and eat cabbage salad flavored with pineapple juice.

"I might be getting married."

"Omigoodness! When?"

"Maybe February. I don't know. I did not think I was going to get married, and now I do. But I don't know."

"Will you still go to school for cooking?"

"Yes."

"Will you live with his family?"

"No! I will still live here. I will just go back to my home every weekend to see him."

"Does he have his own home?"

"No."

"He lives with his parents?"

"Yes."

"You would not live with his parents?"

"Oh no," she shakes her head emphatically. Her body curls up in a tight roll.

"So you won't live together until after you are finished school?"

"Right. But we will see each other on weekends!"

"Wow."

"I just better not get pregnant." She giggles again.

"Would you have to move in with his parents?"

"Ohhhh…" She avoids the question.

"Do you have protection?"

"Ummmm, some people have the, um, the condoms. And some girls are on a medicine. But I don't have anything."

"I see."

"Those things you have in the fridge…" she quickly changes the subject, "the small pieces…"

"The film?"

"Yes, you will send me the ones of me?"

"Of course. Do you have an email? I can send you images online first."

"No. You can send them to Renae."

"Ok. Do you know how to type?"

"Sort of."

"Do you type like this?" I point my index finger at fake points in the air.

"Yes!" She giggles again.

"Do you want to learn how to type?"

"Yes."

"Ok, tomorrow I will show you."

Kukuwa stops sweeping the next morning for a brief lesson. She watches me intently as I indicate the correct way to position the fingers over the keys. Each of her fingers cover the area of two keys. She slowly types CAT, HELLO, and OPHELIA ARTHUR, her given name.

goodbye

Each morning a perfect pearl-shaped sun appears amid the grey. At sunset it becomes amber…

Jeeeeeesus… bless us Jeeeesus….

Traces of the season are popping up amidst the bustle and dust. Stores sell gift baskets of crackers and tropical fruit juice. Heart-shaped plastic packages of chocolates and nuggets are scattered beside plantain chips and digestive biscuits. Shiny tinsel proclaims "Merry Christmas" in front of the Melcom department store.

Old men sell stuffed animals lined in neat rows on a cotton blanket. Young boys heave a wheeled cart of flour sacks up a hill. A man presses his back against the weight. His muscles bulge in dark, shiny mounds. A woman in leopard print spandex chops a whole pineapple for 2000 cedis. She works the machete like a wood carver, swinging the blade in swift rhythm. Taxis sit bumper to bumper at a red light. Celine Dion blasts from the car stereo, "…and so this is Christmas…"

And So This Is Christmas

THERE IS A CHILL IN THE AIR. DUST SITS LIKE FOG, FILLING THE STREETS AND HIDING THE SEA. THE HARMANTTON HAS SET IN.

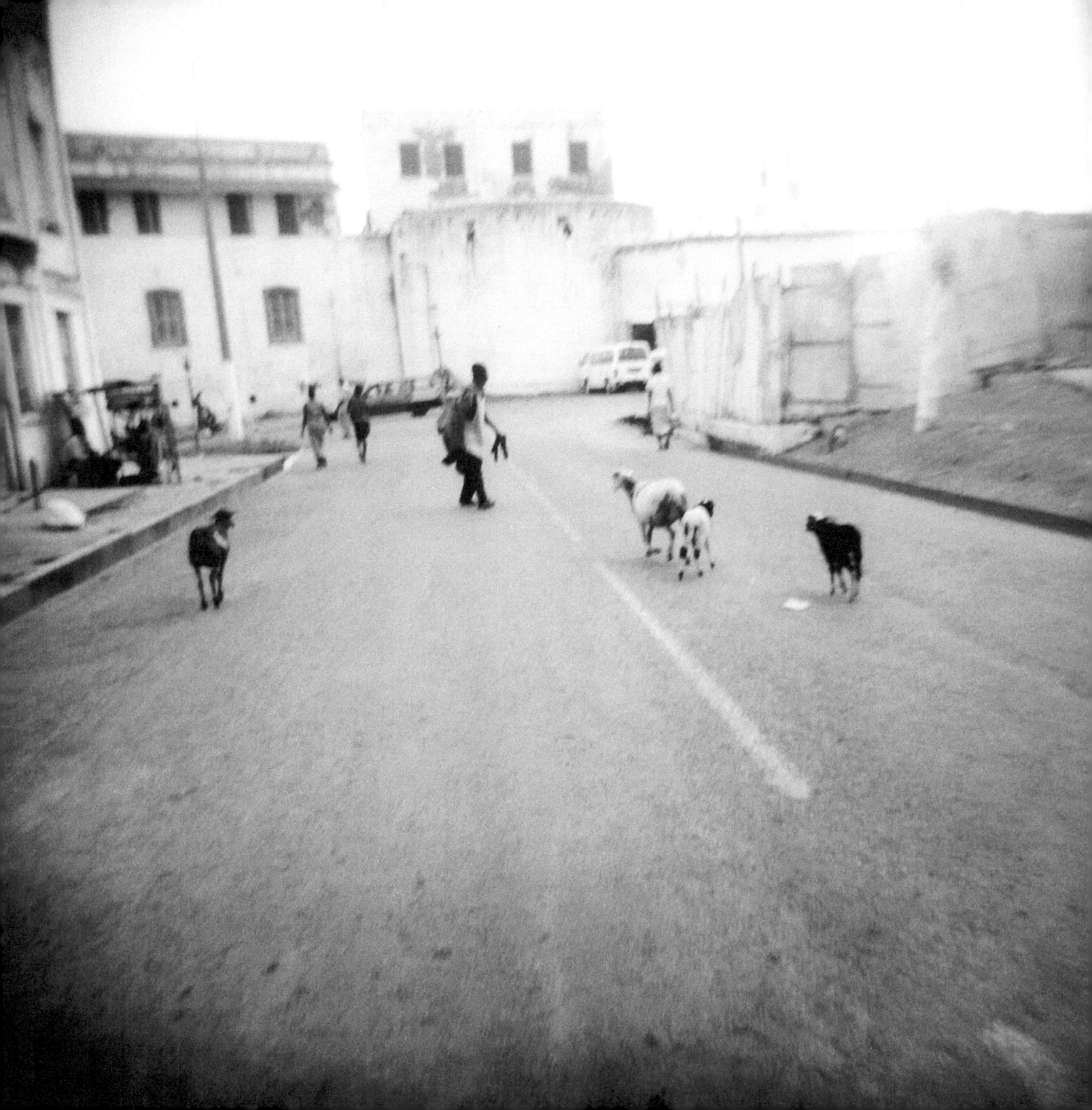

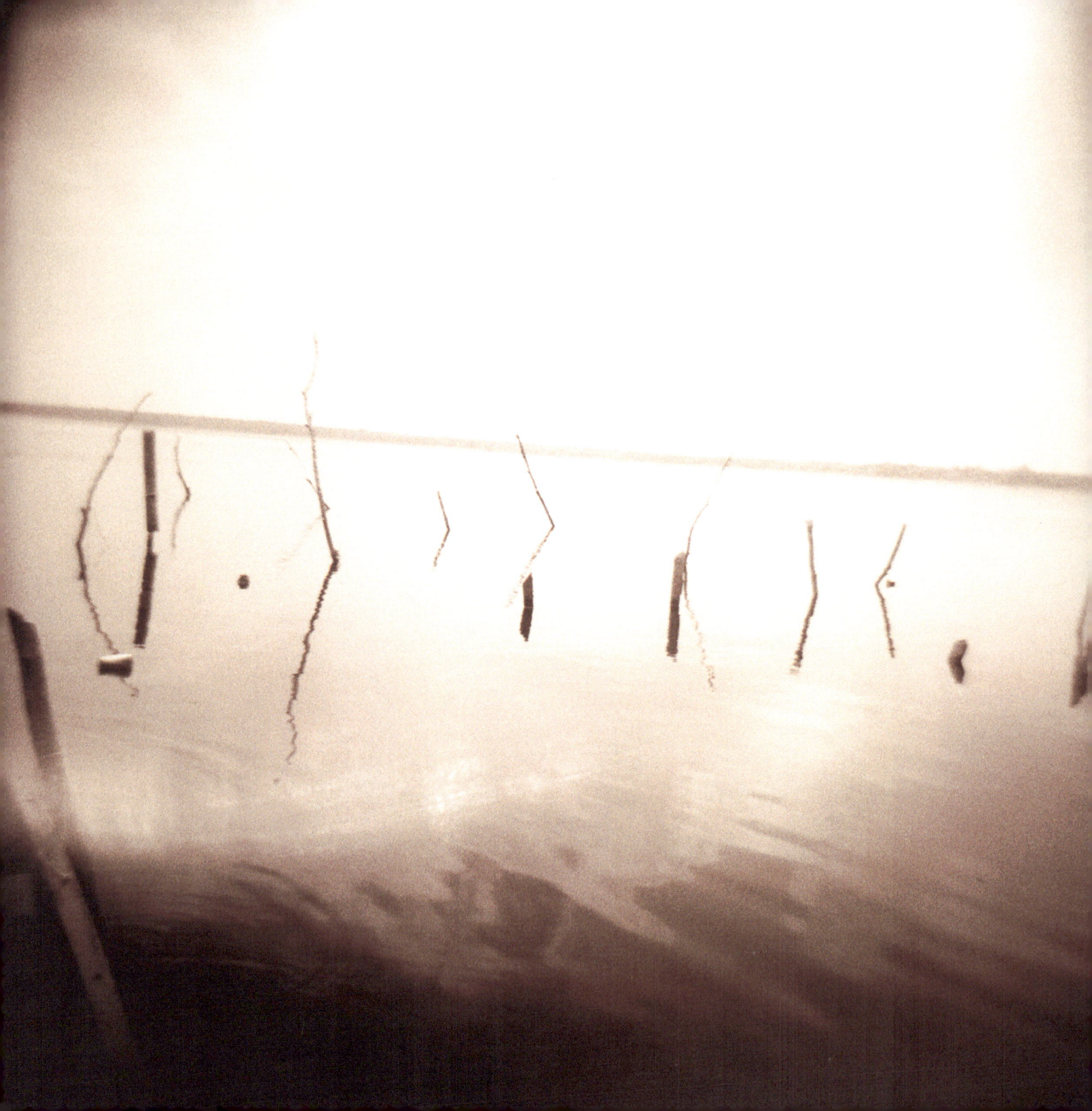

Seaside Holiday

I devote the holiday to swinging in a hammock near the ocean and collecting pearl shells. Nearby, volunteers from England working with a program called "Raleigh" spread out across a long table. They congregate around banana pancakes and Spanish omelets each morning.

At night, a chef from Togo prepares local fish and coconut curries. Men roll pot in plantain leaves and light a huge bonfire on the sand. They beat drums and chant in drunk rhythm. The next morning I leave for Cape Coast early in a ramshackle car bursting with English accents.

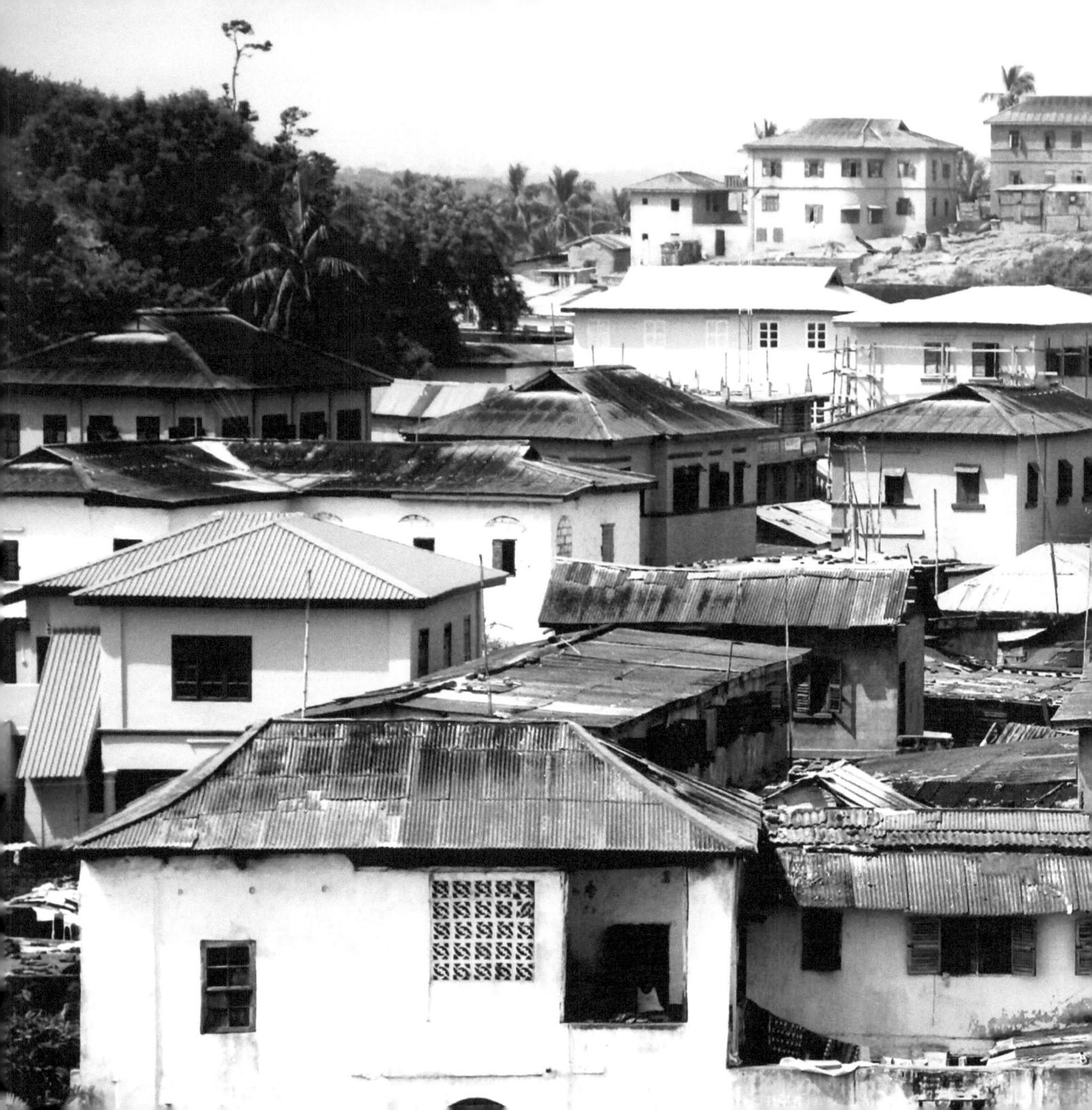

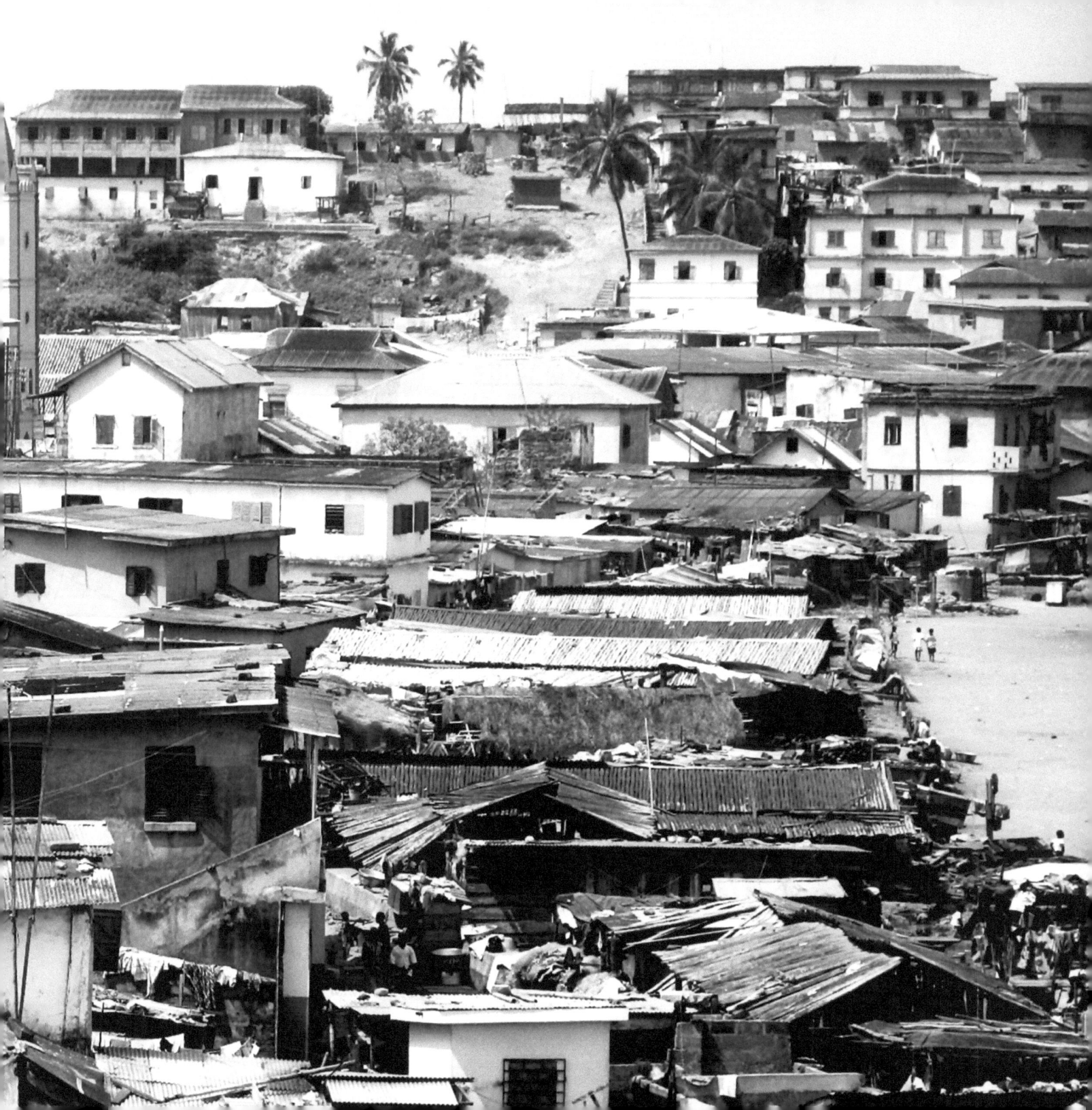

You Will Come Back

A woman dances into church. Decadently dressed in black and white, she waves her arms in the air. Gospel music surrounds the isolated street. Inside a dark room, colorfully printed bodies sway back and forth.

Eli cooks a grand going away meal of groundnut soup, sticky rice balls, salads, and fried plantains. I cook too. Once the meal is over Kukuwa arrives with my specialty, frozen bananas with chocolate powder. Eli sets the food on a lace curtain in buffet style to make room for a tub-sized bowl of groundnut soup.

Eli spends my last night sick in bed. Her body had started aching a few days ago. Now her eyes are puffed shut. She creeps around her café slowly for an anti-climactic goodbye.

KUKUWA ARRIVES WITH MY SPECIALTY, FROZEN BANANAS WITH CHOCOLATE POWDER. I UNCORK A SOUTH AFRICAN CHARDONNAY THAT I WON IN ACCRA.

"You will come back," she murmurs before slumping back into bed.

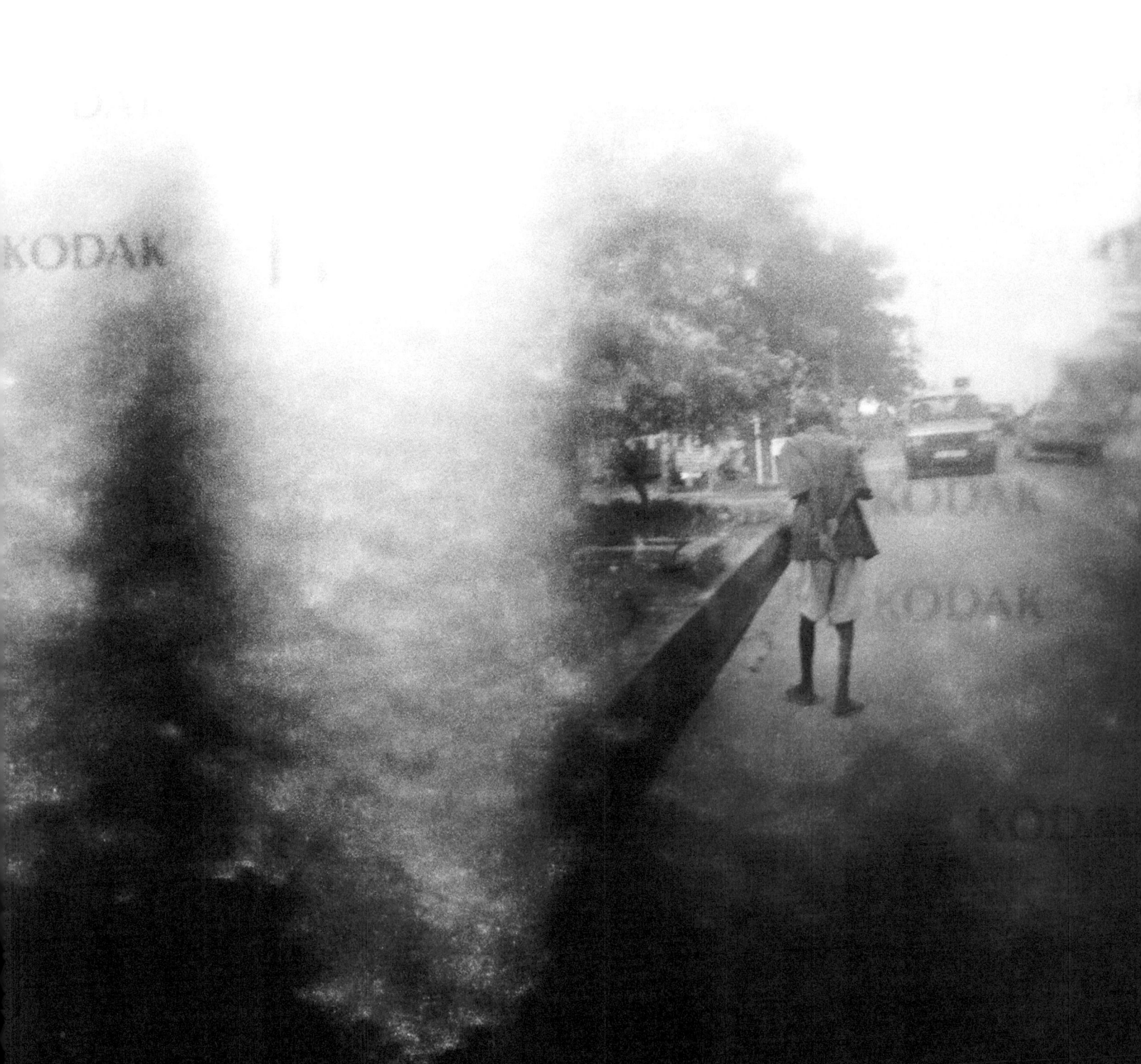

*Hey yahhhhhh… hey yahhhhhhh…*Muslim chants play for a final 4am show… *Hey yahhhhhh… hey yahhhhhhh.*

Pale light filters into the room… tro tro horns echo around crowing roosters….

Hey yahhhhh… hey yahhhhhhh….

WomenInProgress.org

Women in Progress helps women achieve economic independence and alleviate
poverty at a grassroots level. The organization works in developing nations to acheive the
sustainable growth of small, women-owned businesses, and at the same time establishes
mutual understanding among people of diverse cultures.

Global Mamas.org

Global Mamas enhances the international marketplace with unique, high quality,
handmade apparel. Global Mamas also provides sustainable livelihoods for women and
girls in Africa, reduces the economic inequality of African women, and significantly
increases the revenues of participating woman-owned businesses. Global Mamas believes
that helping women gain economic independence is the most effective way to reduce
dependence on foreign aid and steadily create a prosperous society.

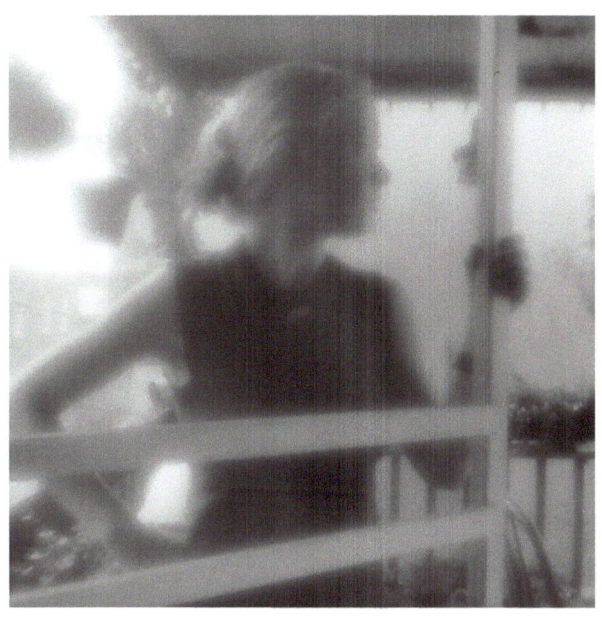

about the author

JULIA'S IMAGES CAPTURE INTIMATE MOMENTS BETWEEN FAMILIES, STRANGERS, TRAVELERS AND WORKERS, WHILE AT THE SAME TIME PRODUCING CANDID LANDSCAPES AND CITYSCAPES.

JULIABLAUKOPF.COM

Julia Blaukopf is an artist, photographer and social documentarian. She has worked as a creative partner with organizations and businesses in Copenhagen, Kenya, Ghana, Lithuania, Montreal and throughout the US. In 2005, Julia worked with a community-run reforestation project in Kenya. A year later she traveled back to Africa to photograph for the Ghanaian organization Women in Progress. In the summer of 2009 Julia set off for Lithuania to photograph the Summer Literary Seminars, a two week writing workshop sponsored by Concordia University in Montreal. In 2010, Julia photographed creatives at work throughout Germany, where she was awarded a visiting artist fellowship at Franz Mayer of Munich. Julia has also traveled extensively in the United States, focusing her lens on women artisans and their work in the creative sector.

Julia worked with Women in Progress as a photographer and a liaison to help promote the women's craft in the U.S. Her goal is to create artistic work that promotes social and political efforts, to create images that embody the mission of Women in Progress, and to help raise awareness for the women artisans' crafting businesses through batiking, sewing, and bead making.

Julia received her Bachelor's in photography from the University of the Arts in Philadelphia and has exhibited her work in Munich and Copenhagen, as well as nationally, in New York, Philadelphia, Baltimore, and Portland, Oregon. She has been honored with the Center for Emerging Visual Artists' Travel Grant, the New Courtland Fellowship, the First Person Arts Fellowship, the Center for Emerging Artists Fellowship, The Camera Club of New York Resident Artist Award, the Oregon College of Art & Craft Resident

Photographer's Award, Marymount College Resident Photography Award, and most recently, Resident Artist Awards at LegalArt in Miami and Artist Residencies Enschede in Holland.

Publications include *PDN Magazine, Metro Philadelphia, The Philadelphia Inquirer, The Philadelphia Weekly,* and *Philadelphia Magazine* in which Julia was chosen as one of Philadelphia's "Artists to Watch".

Julia's photographs create an alternative documentary of the human condition and help bring public attention to noteworthy non-profits, ethically-minded businesses, educational institutions, and public art ventures.

In 2010, Julia launched Julia Pearl, Imprinted Images, LLC, an arts-products venture that pushes the boundaries to re-envision the possibilities for social art and photo-based products.

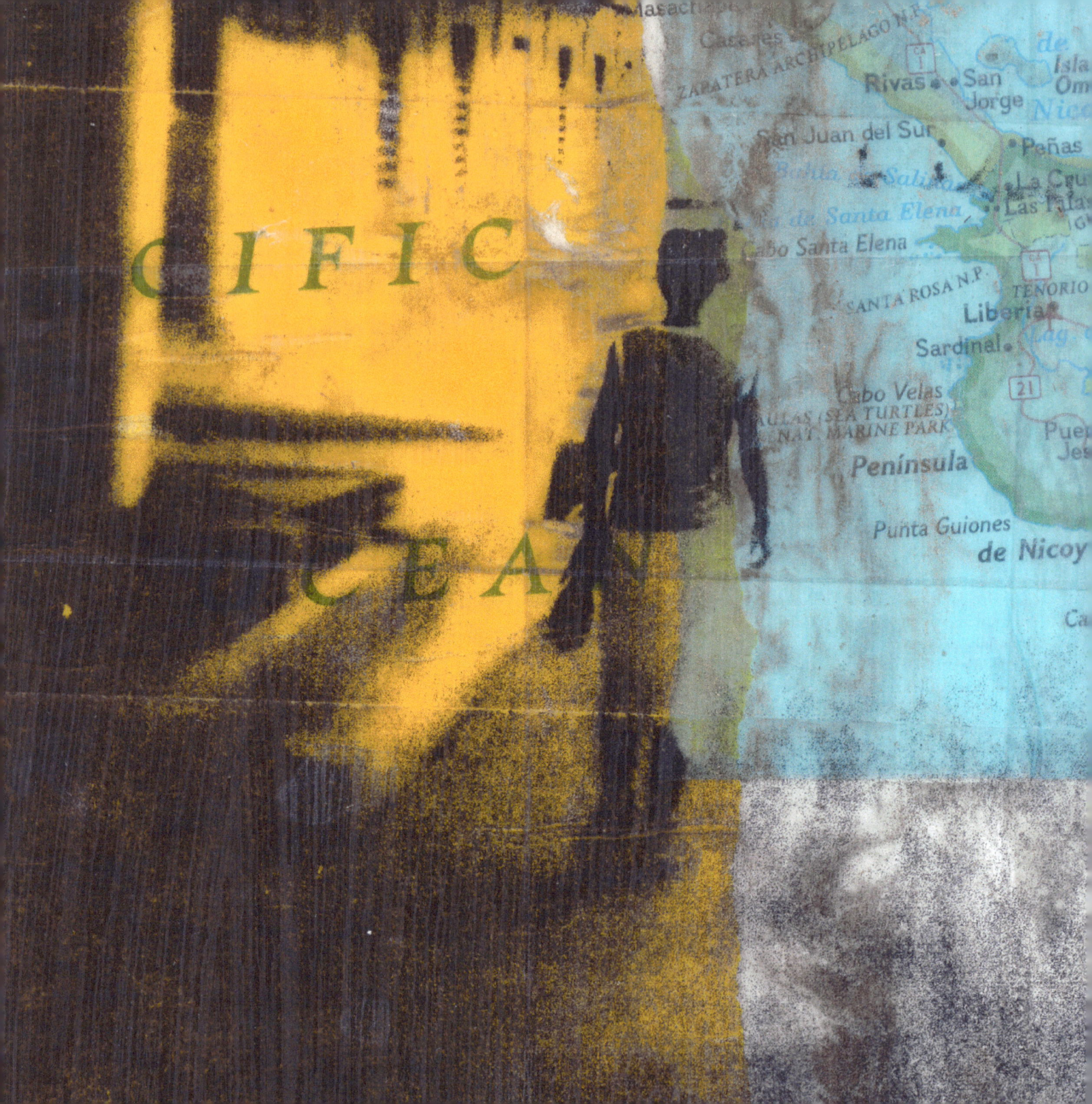

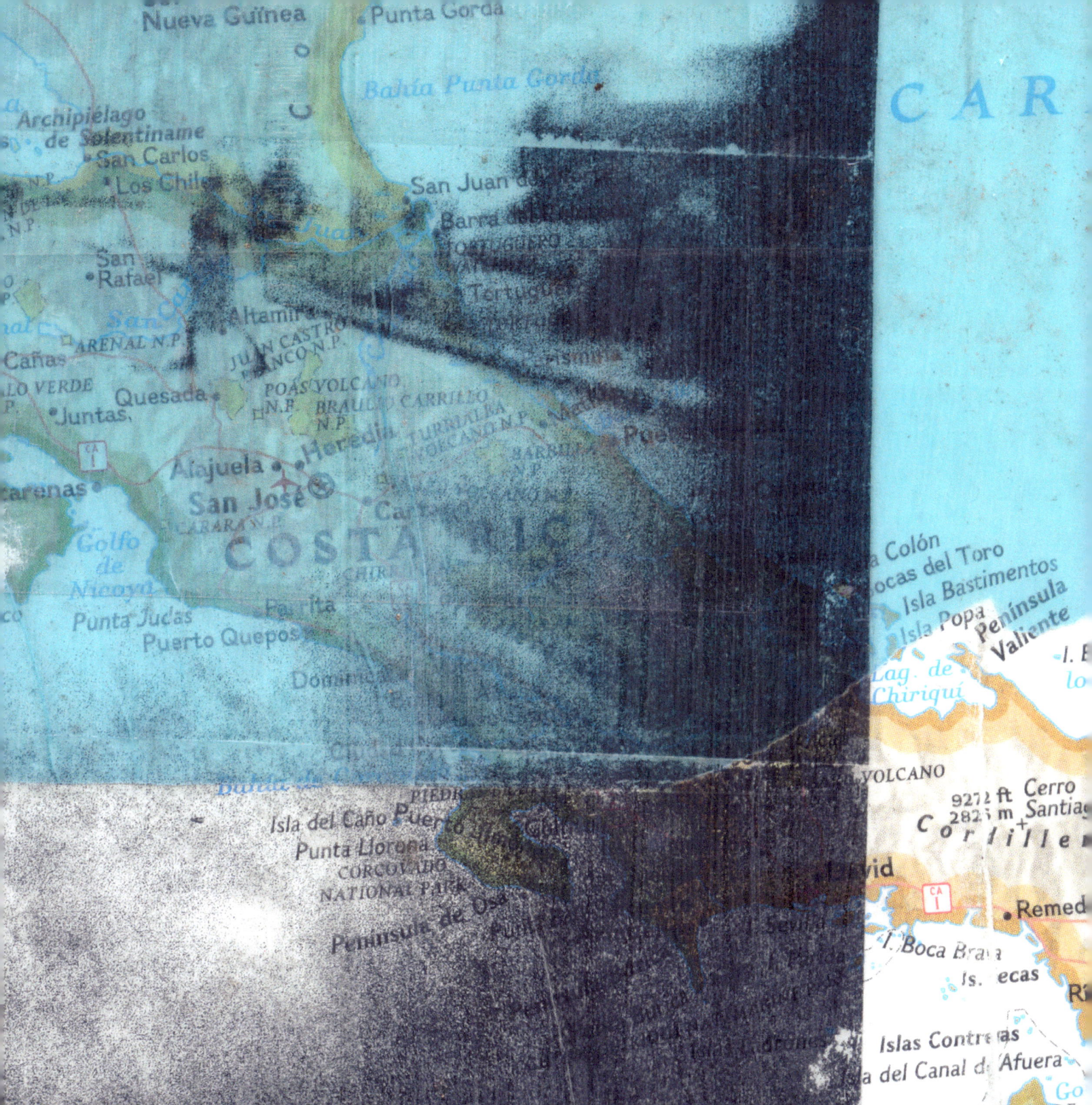

www.ingramcontent.com/pod-product-compliance
Lightning Source LLC
Chambersburg PA
CBHW050849180526
45159CB00007B/2619